Is There a Better Structure for News Providers?

The Potential in Charitable and Trust Ownership

Edited by David A. L. Levy and Robert G. Picard

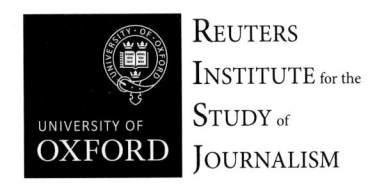

REUTERS INSTITUTE for the STUDY of JOURNALISM
UNIVERSITY OF OXFORD

Contents

PART I: THE ROLES OF CHARITIES AND TRUSTS IN NEWS ORGANISATIONS

1. Why Look at Charitable and Trust Ownership of News Organisations?
   DAVID A. L. LEVY — 3

2. Charitable Ownership and Trusts in News Organisations
   ROBERT G. PICARD — 17

3. Regional Press Challenges Promote Calls for New Ownership Forms and Legal Bases
   NEIL FOWLER — 31

PART II: CASE STUDIES

4. Protecting the *Guardian* through the Scott Trust
   VICTOR KEEGAN — 57

5. Sustaining Independent Journalism through the 'Reuters Trust' (Thomson Reuters Founders Share Company)
   LEONARD BERKOWITZ — 67

6. The Poynter Institute Preserves the *St Petersburg Times*
   KAREN DUNLAP — 73

7. Finding a Way to Protect the Principles of the *Toronto Star*
   JOHN HONDERICH — 79

8. Ensuring Independence at *Ouest-France*
   JEANNE-EMMANUELLE GAPSYS-HUTIN — 85

9. Non-Profit Journalism Entrepreneurialism in the United States
   CHUCK LEWIS — 97

PART III: IMPLICATIONS OF OWNERSHIP

10. Conversations — 115

11. What we Now Know about Charitable and Trust Ownership of News Organisations
    DAVID A. L. LEVY AND ROBERT G. PICARD — 131

Biographies of Authors and Commentators — 137

PART I

THE ROLES OF CHARITIES AND TRUSTS IN NEWS ORGANISATIONS

1. Why look at Charitable and Trust Ownership of News Organisations?

David A. L. Levy

The current problems afflicting news organisations in many parts of the West are leading to a resurgence of interest in alternative forms of ownership and control of those organisations. Faced with what looks like a crisis of the traditional business model it is not surprising that policy-makers, media commentators, and those who are concerned about the future of the democratic role of the press are drawn to examine the alternatives. What is surprising though is the relative paucity of detailed information about some of the alternative arrangements that do exist, together with a full understanding of their diversity, as well as of their relative strengths and weaknesses. This book, which emerges out of a conference held by the Reuters Institute in September 2010, is designed as at least in part to address that lack of information, and to equip those who are drawn to consider alternative forms of ownership and organisation with a more international and reliable evidence base on which to consider the range of options and make policy and commercial choices.

These forms of ownership and operation differ fundamentally from other forms – proprietorships, partnerships, and publicly traded companies – in that they are created for purposes other than being business endeavours producing news products. They are specifically operated to pursue social, political, and cultural goals, guided by the principles and values of those who established them and those who are following in their footsteps. These enterprises can be commercial as well as not-for-profit organisations and vary greatly in size.

No book of this kind can claim to be exhaustive and the cases offered here cover a relatively limited number of cases from a small number of Western countries, primarily the UK, US, Canada and France along with some broader international comparative overviews. Nevertheless we believe that together the detailed analysis, case studies and discussion provided here can help with the current debate and that the mix of academic analysis and participant accounts of various trust and charitable news organisations will prove illuminating and reveal the range of ownership options that exist. Rather than providing a recap of the key points made by each contributor this introduction will aim to situate the current debate within the context of the current economic challenges facing news organisations, the policy debate over the future of news (largely in the UK) and the recent work of the Reuters Institute in this area, as well as highlighting some of the key points that any reader might want to bear in mind as they consider the case studies examined here.

The economic pressures prompting the current debate

As noted above it is largely the economic pressures that are being experienced in many Western countries that are prompting the current resurgence of interest in trust and charitable and other forms of ownership of news organisations. This context is important because it colours perspectives of the challenges facing journalism and desires for alternative ownership solutions. This is an area where the Reuters Institute has already conducted a great deal of research, both on the situation in the UK (Currah, 2009a) and in looking at comparisons between countries as diverse as the US, UK, France, Finland, Germany, India and Brazil (Levy and Nielsen, 2010). What emerges from this research is that while there are considerable challenges, whether one looks nationally or indeed internationally there is neither a uniform picture of crisis – media industries in some emerging economies are doing well – nor a single kind of crisis affecting different countries, nor even a single crisis within countries that are experiencing overall decline in their industries – since the picture may differ markedly between, say local and national newspapers.

There is neither a uniform picture of crisis ... nor a single kind of crisis affecting different countries, nor even a single crisis within countries

The diversity of situations is worth reflecting on if only because it suggests that if there are diverse things occurring within and between different news industries there is unlikely to be a single solution – whether that involves charitable and trust ownership or other approaches.

OECD figures for newspaper publishing revenues between 2007 and 2009 reflect this diversity. True, in the developed world the picture is generally one of decline, but there is a marked difference between the decline of 30% in the US and of 21% in the UK, compared to the figures of 17% in Canada, 10% in Germany, 4% in France, and the growth of 9% in India in the same period (Levy and Nielsen, 2010).

The resilience of these industries to cope with such declines also differs greatly, in part depending on previous profitability (where many US papers had operated at 20% profit or more in the early part of this century and average profits in the UK were still at 19% in 2007) but also in terms of levels of debt, where some industries had accumulated debts in good times that rendered them particularly vulnerable to the subsequent downturn. So amidst the concern about decline we need to see it in historical context, bearing in mind both where the industry has come from and how resilient it is likely to prove in a recession.

What is clear is that recession, where it has occurred, has been tough, has tended to feed through pretty fast to a round of job cutting, and in the US and UK has impacted fastest on local and regional news organisations. Michael Schudson's assessment of how the erosion of profits has played out across US newspapers makes for pretty chilling reading:

> . . . newspapers have slashed their budgets, closed foreign bureaux and statehouse bureaux, reduced the number of days a week they print the paper, and in the space of a half dozen years have laid off or bought out a quarter to a third of all newspaper reporters, editors, and news photographers, from new recruits to Pulitzer Prize winners. In the space of a few years the number of journalists employed in newsrooms of daily papers around the country has been reduced from just over 60,000 to somewhere in the 40,000s, probably at the low end of that (Pew Project for Excellence in Journalism, 2010). The number of reporters stationed full-time in state capitals dropped from 524 in 2003 to 355 in 2009, a decline of a third (Dorroh, 2009). In New Jersey, the number of full-time statehouse reporters dropped from more than fifty to just fifteen in the space of ten years (Starr, 2009: 31). In New York, the Legislative Correspondents Association of journalists who covered the state government in Albany had a membership of fifty-nine reporters from thirty-one news organisations in 1981; this declined to fifty-one journalists from twenty-nine organisations in 2001, down to forty-one journalists from twenty-seven organisations in 2008 (Peters, 2008). (Schudson, 2010)

Arguably the US is unusual in the extent to which its politics is organised at state level and the degree to which the news industry is organised locally and regionally rather than nationally. This makes the impact of the withdrawal from local and state reporting even more serious than elsewhere (Starr, 2009). But the sense of decline –

where it is taking place – being most acute at the regional and local level is replicated across the OECD and the concerns about the impact on democracy extends beyond the US. OECD figures show that the circulation of local newspapers averaged an 8.3% decline between 2004 and 2008 compared to a decline in national newspaper circulation of 2.8% (OECD, 2010).

In the UK, although there is much more of a national market for news – and indeed for politics – the 20% decline in the circulation of paid-for local and regional dailies in the same period is more than double the overall OECD average (OECD 2010). It is also remarkable how much the local rather than the national press has been hit by the transfer of advertising revenue to the internet. Figures from the UK regulator Ofcom show, while total newspaper advertising declined from £5.11bn to £4.12bn between 2004 and 2008, around 80% of this decline hit local rather than national newspapers with the bulk of that decline focused on local classified advertising (see Figure 1.1). This impact of that reduction was all the more significant because UK local papers are heavily reliant on advertising – and often classified advertising – for 79% of their revenues as against UK national papers, where advertising accounts on average for 44% of revenues. (Ofcom, 2009).

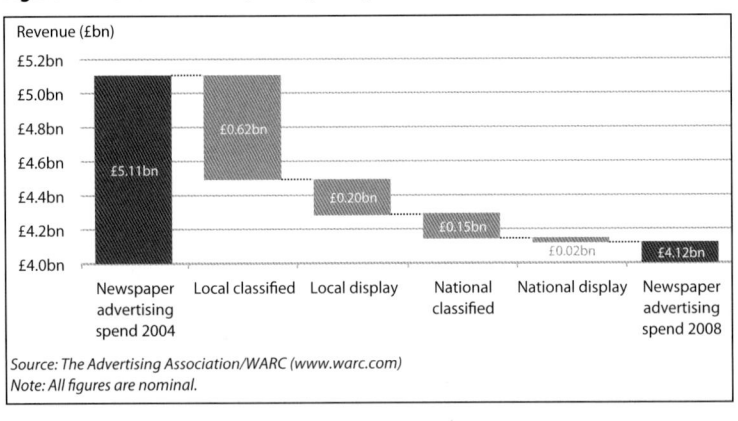

Figure 1.1 Revenue in £bn (Ofcom, 2009)

Newspaper advertising spend 2004	£5.11bn
Local classified	£0.62bn
Local display	£0.20bn
National classified	£0.15bn
National display	£0.02bn
Newspaper advertising spend 2008	£4.12bn

Source: The Advertising Association/WARC (www.warc.com)
Note: All figures are nominal.

As John Lloyd has pointed out in the context of a decline in national newspaper circulation and revenues, the even more rapid impact of these declines on local and regional papers was particularly hard felt, with no sign of respite in sight.

> Regional papers . . . have been closing at a rate of around one a week for the past two years – a trend which is forecast to accelerate. Claire Enders, who runs Enders Analysis, a media consultancy, told the House of Commons Committee on Culture, Media and Sport in June 2009 that half of the

1,300 regional titles would close in the next five years, as some £1.3bn is lost to the industry because of the collapse of the advertising market, and of circulation. (Lloyd, 2010)

The challenges are not merely a result of ownership, however, and involve greater questions of resources necessary to carry out journalism in a democracy. A poorly funded charitably owned news organisation is unlikely to be able to provide the scale and scope of journalism needed by society any more than a commercial one.

Some reflections on the policy debate over the future of news organisations

The problems afflicting the news industry have led to a range of policy initiatives and discussions in different countries, from the Etats Généraux de la Presse convened by President Sarkozy in France in 2008, to the hearings by the Congress and Federal Trade Commission in the US, to the processes undertaken by Ofcom and the UK government that led to the *Digital Britain* report in 2009. This brief discussion touches on the US and looks in a little more detail at the UK. In the US there has been a flurry of generally foundation-funded not for profit news initiatives of the kind examined by Charles Lewis in this book (see Chapter 9). Many of these such as ProPublica and Talking Points Memo have a national focus, are largely targeted at enthusiasts of investigative reporting in politics, or at partisans of one particular point of view; both groups feel that without foundation support their kind of journalism would be endangered.[1] In addition, at the local level some universities have helped by contributing the expertise of their trainee journalists to fill gaps left in local news in their communities as local newspapers either close or wind down their news operations. Finally the decline has led some to call for some public funding to be considered to sustain accountability journalism at the local and state level (Schudson, 2010; and Downie and Schudson, 2009).

In the US talk of direct public funding for any form of news – beyond the limited service already offered by NPR through a mix of Congressional and donor funding – has a habit of stalling even when government budgets are less squeezed than they are at present, since it quickly leads to accusations that public funding will automatically undermine freedom of speech and lead to politically controlled news. However, in recent years US foundation-funded initiatives seem to some extent to have compensated in terms of innovation and funding for the inability of public funding to play a significant role in this debate. In that sense the US is the country par excellence that people turn to when the talk moves to foundation and charitable funding of news. It

---

[1] In this context the recent sale of the Huffington Post to AOL for $315m suggests that in a market the size of the US there are some forms of online news and aggregation that can attract commercial funding.

is important to remember however that the US is probably unique in the scale of private charitable and foundation funding that is devoted to a whole range of activities, whether in education, culture, health and medical activities, and a host of other social activities.

The US is probably unique in the scale of private charitable and foundation funding

The UK debate is framed in a very different way. First, there is the presence of the BBC, which is a £3.5bn intervention in the UK media market. Second, there is the existence of a plurality of public service broadcasters alongside the BBC, with the publically owned but commercially funded Channel 4 as well as ITV and Five, which all have had obligations to broadcast impartial news – and in the case of ITV, local and regional news too. Third, the weakness of UK foundation and charitable funding for news media is the mirror image of its generosity with public funding. No independent UK foundation from outside the sector puts large enough amounts of funding into news production to sustain a news organisation. Finally, the relatively small size of the UK's population – less than 20% that of the US – means that given the high fixed costs of news any charitable funding would need to be relatively much more generous to reach a comparable number of people to those reached by US foundation-funded news.

However, in spite of these differences there are two respects in which the UK debate comes closer to the US one. In both there is a focus on local and regional rather than national news, though the UK debate is about local TV as well as the press rather than simply the press alone.[2] UK print journalists are also, like their US colleagues, for the most part very wary of accepting public funding. This is not because UK journalists believe that public funding must necessarily always lead to political interference – few believe, for example, that BBC journalists are at the beck and call of the government of the day. It is more easily explained by the very different cultures that separate a highly partisan and relatively unregulated press in the UK from a broadcast sector led by the BBC which is relatively highly regulated, and, as noted above, where while all providers are bound by political impartiality rules, arguably the impartiality of BBC journalists is scrutinised most closely because of its public funding.

The UK policy debate about the future of local news gathered pace in 2009. Its origins lay in the analysis by Ofcom of the cyclical and structural pressures facing the provision of local and regional news from ITV, which had for some time been seeking a reduction in its local news obligations,

---

[2] One should not minimise the long-term decline in the UK national press too. The figures for circulation tell a dramatic story. In Nov. 2000 the 10 national UK titles together sold a total of 12,543,510 copies. Ten years later, in Nov. 2010 the same 10 titles sold just 9.844,024 copies – a decline of 22%. Some of the falls were spectacular, with decreases for a newspaper like the Daily Mirror of 45%, The Times 30%, Daily Telegraph 33% and Guardian 31%. (Levy, 2011). See also Lloyd (2010) for a detailed account of the problems facing the UK press.

arguing that its revenues could not cover the costs of the service. Over the following years there were a series of policy initiatives including the development by Ofcom of the idea of Independently Funded News Consortia (IFNCs) at local and regional level where media companies or new entrants or consortia might tender to provide a local TV news service (Barnett, 2010). The Labour government took up this idea and started a tender process for a series of pilots, which was abandoned by the incoming coalition government in May 2010. The policy disagreement was largely about the funding of any solution – where the coalition government favoured a commercial rather than publicly funded approach – but there was agreement about the fundamental policy objective, namely that local news mattered, was in danger, and needed protection. The policy concerns expressed in the Labour government's Digital Britain report of June 2009 remain current:

> *As the economic foundations of news publishers come under great pressure, especially in local and regional markets, there's an imminent danger that large parts of the UK will be left without professionally verified sources of information. Information is the lifeblood of a vibrant economy. A strong, viable and diverse news media is also integral to democratic life. When a newspaper goes under, we lose more than a tax-paying business. We also lose an institution's memory; archives, values and community relationships that have, in many cases, been built through generations. Worst of all, we risk losing the talent of seasoned editors and journalists.* (Dept for Business Innovations and Skills and Dept of Culture, Media and Sport, 2009)

And while the policy solutions proposed by the Digital Britain report were of their time, the general encouragement of not-for-profit and community solutions is not that distant from the subsequent coalition government's advocacy of community solutions as part of their 'Big Society' initiative (see below).

> *To sustain the vital civic function of journalism, citizens, Government and business will need collaboratively to devise new ways of funding the news. The commercial model will continue to play an important role, especially as publishers explore the potential of new platforms and technologies. But it will also need to be supplemented with a range of alternative models – for example, local ownership, community media and non-profit organizations. (Ibid.)*

The interest in not-for-profit solutions was in part fostered by two pieces of work by Andrew Currah for the Reuters Institute in 2009: first, a study of the impact of the internet on UK news organisations published in January 2009 (Currah, 2009a) which floated the idea that not-for-profit solutions and tax breaks might have a role to play, and then a second piece looking in more detail at solutions to the crisis in local news, which was commissioned by Ofcom as part of their analysis of the prospects for local news and TV and which was published in September 2009 (Currah, 2009b). Currah outlined the problem as he saw it:

> *In summary, we believe that it is the intangible, community-focused aspects of journalism that appear to be most at stake in the current media crisis. If local and regional journalism is a vital part of the national media, and a pivotal element of community life and democratic governance, then we need to think openly and dispassionately about ways to address the economics that now threaten its continued survival.* (Currah 2009b)

He went on to outline possible ways in which government might help:

> *a vital and potentially transformative area of government intervention relates to the topic of trust ownership . . . we believe it is worthwhile considering the role government might play in the formation of local and regional news trusts. In theory, these could function as either charitable or non-charitable trusts, initially seeded with public money. The purpose would be to direct an amount of capital into a series of trusts, which would be constitutionally designed to provide arms-length support to local and regional news provision in its myriad forms. . . . Local and regional news trusts could provide transitional funds for news operations facing closure. For example, they could support local business owners, community groups or even staff who wished to acquire a news operation from a commercial owner. This might include legal and technical advice, notably for those wishing to convert a news operation into a charitable body or some variant of community-focused incorporation. In some cases, as we have explained, news operations may fare better outside the prevailing commercial model, not least due to problems of indebtedness and the pressure to create shareholder value.* (Currah, 2009b)

One of the areas that Currah drew attention to was the uncertainty surrounding the treatment of news – both at local and national level – and whether it might qualify for charitable status by the UK Charity Commission. There was a sense that, while other countries such as the US, Canada, and France seemed to have mechanisms for recognising the public purposes of news within legal and fiscal charitable arrangements, the route to these within the UK could be more problematic and needed to be clarified (see Neil Fowler, Chapter 3 below).

However, the broad arguments presented by Currah were pitched into a relatively receptive climate. The UK Carnegie Trust produced a report in 2010 titled *Making Good Society* which included considerable reflection on the role of the media in this task, where in common with others it saw some linkage between insulation from commercial pressures and the quality of local media (eee also Goldsmiths, 2010). Under the heading of 'growing local and community news media' the Carnegie Trust report stated:

> *We want to see policy and financial commitments from local and national governments and support from philanthropic organisations to enhance the infrastructure for local and community media.*

The report drew attention to a particular trend that concerned policy-makers, namely the fact that while the political tendencies – particularly in the devolved nations of Scotland and Wales – were leading towards greater decentralisation of power, the economic pressures on the news industry were working in the opposite direction. The result was a diminution in the original news being generated within those nations, precisely at the moment when devolved decision-making was increasing and required ever greater scrutiny (Gardam and Levy, 2008). English cities and towns were facing similar pressures on their local papers, with some local councils claiming they could fill the gap with a new breed of council-funded newspapers; an innovation that was viewed with scepticism by many, both for commercial and political reasons, and was halted after the election of the coalition government in May 2010. The government then went on to launch a new plan for local television in January 2011, what with it described as 'a new channel dedicated to the provision of local news and content . . . that will sit alongside other public service broadcasters, offering a new voice for local communities, with local perspectives that are directly relevant to them' (Hunt, 2011).

The rationale for the new government's policy was based once again on a restatement of the importance of the local:

> *8 out of 10 people in this country consider local news important. 'Focus on the local area' is consistently ranked as a high priority. . . . Our vision of a connected, big society is one in which we really do value the local as much as the national or international. And local television is one area – perhaps the only area – in which our outstandingly successful media sector has been outstandingly unsuccessful in responding to consumer needs. The painful truth is*

> *that we probably have one of the most centralised media ecologies of any developed country. Think about Sheffield, Bristol, or Birmingham – all major cities that don't have a single local TV station between them. What is good enough for Dublin or Galway, Lyon or Marseille, Catalonia or Calgary, is certainly good enough for them. And if we want to be the best, we should settle for no less.* (Hunt, 2011)

These ideas were reinforced by the Prime Minister, David Cameron, in a message of support that he offered for local newspaper week in May 2011, where he said (cited by Roy Greenslade[3]):

> *Local newspapers are hugely important to our country – for two good reasons. First, they strengthen our democracy, holding the powerful to account.*
> *Whereas national newspapers can focus on the bigger picture, it's local papers that often really analyse the detail of what central and local government is doing and the impact their policies have on the ground.*
> *Second, local papers are hugely important in helping to build a bigger, stronger society. There is a massive gap between the state on the one hand, and the individual on the other, and local papers help fill the space in between, galvanising readers into action.*

The discussions and debates about the importance of journalism and the status of news organisations reveal deep belief in their importance to society and it is this belief that is spurring efforts to find solutions to the contemporary challenges.

The relevance of trust and charitable ownership to the current debate

Returning to the overall debate over charitable and trust ownership, there does seem to be a strong argument for reviewing not-for-profit or non-profit-seeking structures at a time when commercial circumstances for news are tough, particularly in local news. New forms of ownership potentially offer some degree of protection, both from cyclical declines in the market and from the short-termism imposed by commercial investors preferring an increase in immediate profits even at the cost of compromising the quality of the journalism that often underpins the long-term survival of the news organisation.

But there is a paradox here. Among the many striking facts that emerge from the case studies examined in this book is that many of

---
[3] www.guardian.co.uk/media/greenslade/2011/may/12/davidcameron-local-newspapers (consulted May 2011).

the most successful arrangements studied here were created at a time of commercial success rather than weakness. Often the charitable or trust arrangements documented here were devised precisely to protect a profitable company from those seeking to take it over, or use it for purposes other than those that the founders or controllers desired. But their ability to design such arrangements was often based on a position of commercial strength, combined with individual or collective generosity in terms of accepting lower rates of return today and in the future than in a purely market-based and tradable company. The extent to which this marked difference in context matters depends in part on the predictions for the long-term health of the news industry. It seems likely that trust and charitable arrangements created at times of a structural rather than simply cyclical weakness in the news market – and at least in part to redress the pressures exercised by that weakness – will either require a higher rate of investment or the creation of a new business model if they are to be self-sustaining over the long term.

Many of the successful arrangements studied here were created at a time of commercial success rather than weakness

Therein lies the potential opportunity for experiments with charitable and trust ownership conceived in times of adversity. Many of the cases studied in this book saw their ownership structure changed in order to preserve something that as well as being profitable was thought to fulfil a special purpose. Philanthropy aimed at preservation of this kind is admirable and may deliver many benefits. But it also contains risks, of organisations that outgrow their founder's vision, that find the charitable or trust arrangements they have been bequeathed ill adapted to changing circumstances, or that use the financial insulation provided by past profits to resist necessary adaptation. Most of the cases examined in this book have found ways to adapt to new circumstances, and are often at the forefront of their sector. But if there is a danger in structures primarily focused on preservation, then that may be a risk that is easier to avert when new structures are created in times of crisis than of prosperity. People considering new charitable and trust structures today will inevitably be asking harder questions about the long-term financial sustainability of the venture than might have been the case in the past when it seemed as if an ever expanding supply of advertising would go on paying for news forever. In those circumstances sometimes it seemed as if financial sustainability might look after itself, with trust structures focused on what was then seen as the main problem, that of ownership and control.

In that context it is interesting that many of the new US experiments with foundation-funded journalism are generally targeted at the creation of a new entity rather than saving an existing news organisation in difficulty. The same applies to the UK's pioneering Bureau of Investigative Journalism based at City University, established through the generosity of the David and Elaine Potter Foundation. But while, as noted above, arrangements of this kind have great potential for creating first-class journalism, they may be harder to secure in smaller markets, with a less well developed tradition of philanthropy than in the US. And all of these initiatives may have trouble sustaining themselves if the initial donor's commitment or other funding runs out. But what remains interesting about them is that because they are conceived in times of difficulty and are genuinely completely new they are more focused on trying to invent a new business model as a way to secure their long-term future rather than simply preserving the past.

Local and community news is one of the areas attracting greatest thought about new forms of ownership. It is also an area where there is arguably the liveliest debate about new ways of providing news that reaches the whole community as opposed to simply a particular group within it. The relationship between the quality of local news and the quality of local democracy requires further examination but it seems fair to assume that there is a connection between the two both at national and local level. However it is at the local level that the threats are greatest, since the economies of scale that can pay for quality reporting are hardest to secure in the smaller markets. For that reason local news will be one of the areas that will continue to attract most interest for the potential of alternative forms of charitable and trust ownership to guarantee their future provision and quality.

We hope that people considering that area, as well as others, find many useful examples and lessons to draw on in this book. Our comparative and international focus is no accident. Rather it stems from our view that media policy debates are too often framed within a narrow national perspective. Every country's media system is unique and framed in part by its history. But at a time of rapid change in almost every aspect of the news industry we believe that there is a value in looking beyond national borders in the search for policy as well as practical lessons. This book, and the conference on which it was based, is produced in that spirit. We hope that it helps create some new thinking in the debate about the future of news and the relationship between the quality of our media and the quality of democracy. Alternative structures such as trust and charitable ownership are an important part of that debate and to date have attracted insufficient study.

References

Barnett, Steven (2010) 'Minding the Regional News Gap', *British Journalism Review*, 21(1): 13–18.

Commission of Inquiry into the future of Civil Society in the UK and Ireland (2010) *Making Good Society* (Dunfermline: Carnegie UK Trust).

Currah, Andrew (2009) *What's Happening to Our News: An Investigation into the Likely Impact of the Digital Revolution on the Economics of News Publishing in the UK* (Oxford: Reuters Institute for the Study of Journalism).

— (2009b) *Navigating the Crisis in Local and Regional News: A Critical Review of Solutions* (Oxford: Reuters Institute).

Department for Business Innovations and Skills and Department of Culture, Media and Sport (2009) *Digital Britain* (London: HMSO).

Downie, L., and Schudson, M. (2009) *The Reconstruction of American Journalism* (New York: Columbia University Graduate School of Journalism).

Gardam, T., and Levy, D. A. (2008) *The Price of Plurality* (Oxford: Reuters Institute).

Goldsmiths Leverhulme Media Research Centre (2010) *Meeting the News Needs of Local Communities* (London: Media Trust).

Hunt, J. (19 Jan. 2011) Retrieved May 2011, from www.culture.gov.uk/news/ministers_speeches/7726.aspx.

Levy, D. A. (2011) 'Beyond Fatalism? New Perspectives on Public Interest Journalism', *Nordicom-Information*, 3–24.

— and Nielsen, R. K. (2010) *The Changing Business of Journalism and its Implications for Democracy* (Oxford: Reuters Institute).

Lloyd, J. (2010) 'The Press We Destroy', in D. A. Levy and R. K. Nielsen (eds), *The Changing Business of Journalism and its Implications for Democracy* (Oxford: Reuters Institute), 81–94.

OECD (2010) *News in the Internet Age: New Trends in News Publishing* (Paris: OECD).

Ofcom (2009) *Communications Market Review* (London: Ofcom).

Schudson, M. (2010) 'News in Crisis in the United States: Panic – and Beyond', in D. A. Levy and R. K. Nielsen (eds), *The Changing Business of Journalism and its Implications for Democracy* (Oxford: Reuters Institute), 95–106.

Starr, P. (2009) 'Goodbye to the Age of Newspapers (Hello to a New Era of Corruption)', *New Republic* (4 Mar.).

2. Charitable Ownership and Trusts in News Organisations

Robert G. Picard

The contemporary strategic and financial crises facing newspapers throughout the Western world has led to concern about how to fund journalism in the twenty-first century and how to ensure that citizens continue to receive the information necessary to carry out civic activities in a democracy (Currah, 2009; Pickard et al., 2009; Reilly Center, 2008). This has produced increasing interest in alternative structures of news organisation ownership and operation.

The diminished effectiveness of dominant business models, news company redundancies, insolvencies, and obvious gaps in coverage have led many to focus on existing examples of alternative structures, such as the *Guardian* and *Observer* (Akst, 2005; Schiffrin, 2007; Weisberg, 2009). Government reviews, such as the Ofcom review of local and regional news in the UK, suggest that 'new models of ownership may have a bigger role to play in enabling newspaper owners and other interested parties to continue trading while delivering social aims. . . . Examples include charitable and non-charitable trusts and community interest companies' (Ofcom, 2009: 10). Across the Atlantic a study of developments in the United States identified similar needs for new forms of not-for-profit operations and even subsidies to make if news organisations are to be sustainable (Downie and Schudson, 2010) and – after several hearings on the problems of news provision – the staff at the US Federal Trade Commission saw similar needs to establish new organisational forms and operations (US Federal Trade Commission, 2010).

A great deal of interest has been generated in trusts and other forms of not-for-profit ownership, but many discussions of alternatives tend to group together ownership forms or governance arrangements that are different from traditional commercial enterprises and there is little understanding of the significant differences in purposes and structures among them.

Consequently, proponents of alternative forms of ownership and control tend to be highly enthusiastic and exhibit superficial understanding of the nature of the structures, their operations, and their challenges. Some commentators express utopian visions that such arrangements create journalism without financial concerns, arguing that journalism can be independent only through non-profit ownership (Loundy, 2007) and that such arrangements have been said to give the *Guardian* 'the freedom to lose money' (Weisberg, 2009).

Proponents of alternative forms of ownership and control tend to be highly enthusiastic and exhibit superficial understanding of the nature of the structures, their operations, and their challenges

The latter observation was made without regard to the fact that the Guardian was experiencing losses of £100,000 a day and that its managing director had written to its staff admitting that 'We are looking at everything – literally everything – that we do so see how we can economise. . . . However, because the biggest portion of our costs is people's salaries, we have to review staffing levels' (Andrews, 2009). The Scott Trust, which owns the *Guardian*, was also wrestling with the future of its sister, the *Observer*, and was considering closing the 200-year-old paper because it had not produced a profit in the seventeen years it had been owned by Guardian Media Group and had losses of £90m (*The Times*, 2009). The trust changed its ownership and control form to that of a limited company in 2008 to gain more leeway in dealing with tax and other challenges of contemporary operations (Conlan, 2008; Guardian Media Group, 2008).

Earlier concerns about ownership

Most discussion of the need for alternative ownership sees the necessity as a unique and contemporary development. The contemporary situation, however, is not the first time that discussions about the creation of trusts and charitable arrangements have arisen.

In the UK, for example, the Royal Commission on the Press (1947–9) saw trusts as a means to reduce commercial pressures and urged additional state support be given to them (Royal Commission, 1949). It did so because of newspaper closures and because developments in the United Kingdom led proprietors of a number of British newspapers and news organisations to begin setting up trusts. These legal arrangements put papers in the hands of trustees and obliged them to operate them in particular ways, usually preserving standards, traditions, and political attitudes.

These trusts, however, could be private or charitable, with charitable trusts' income exempt from many taxes. It was noted that creating a trust does not

> *automatically convert a newspaper from a commercial to a non-commercial concern. . . . Even an ownership trust may merely substitute for the private shareholder some other person or cause to whose interests the profits are to be devoted, and the newspaper may still be run with the object of making profits (Political and Economic Planning, 1959: 151)*

During the 1950s and 1960s economies of scale in procurement and production were insufficient to save many segments of the British press from financial challenges involving inflation, taxation, and labour demands, leading to closures and consolidations. Politically active press barons who were selling their national or regional papers turned to trust arrangement to try to preserve some of the political leanings of their papers as they were sold to larger conglomerates.

Trust arrangements were also considered a way to reduce commercial pressures on the press and editorial interference, and the Royal Commission on the Press argued that

> *the formation of trusts – and particularly of trusts safeguarding the independence of the editor – should be encouraged by giving taxation benefits to undertakings so owned. Some witnesses believed that trust ownership was free from the excessive commercialism attributed to large-scale private ownership and allowed greater independence of the editor. (Royal Commission, 1949: 151)*

Trust arrangements were considered a way to reduce commercial pressures on the press and editorial interference

Although some observers saw trusts as a way of protecting editors from commercial, political or cultural interference, one study noted that they do not necessarily ensure editorial independence because 'trust provisions may limit the editor's freedom of action and control the editorial policy to be followed rather than enhance his status and independence' (*Political and Economic Planning*, 1959: 137). A particularly important challenge identified was ensuring that trust-owned papers are properly governed, noting the difficulty of any firm finding suitable board members. The problem is magnified in trusts because 'the trustees must give their time more or less for love; there is not worthwhile financial reward' (ibid. 155).

Whether trusts could be used to promote establishment of entry news organisations was unclear, the researchers said. 'With the necessary financial backing it might be possible to create a new paper with trust provisions, but this would not guarantee its success, quality, or character' (ibid. 157).

Charitable structures of newspapers have received far less attention than trusts in the UK, undoubtedly because they are few in number, do not involve larger publications, and the public interest functions of news organisations are not explicitly recognised in charities legislation.

Understanding the range of ownership and control possibilities, and the opportunities and challenges they present, are crucial if discussions about their potential for ameliorating contemporary problems in news provision are to shift from debate to action. To bridge the gap of knowledge about charitable and trust owned media, I want to turn attention to some of the differences among existing news organisations that employ such structures.

Understanding organisational structures

If one considers the structures of charitable and trust owned media, three major forms of alternative ownership and control are apparent: (1) charitable ownership and control, in which news organisations are owned and controlled by a charitable organisation; (2) charitably supported media, in which organisations receive support from charities and charitable individuals; and (3) trust ownership and control, in which news organisations are owned or controlled by trust arrangements for purposes of supporting quality journalism.

Charitable ownership and control

Charitable ownership and control involves a structural arrangement in which a charity owns a news organisation. In such arrangements, the news organisation may be a not-for-profit enterprise – as in the case of the *Christian Science Monitor* – or it may be a for-profit enterprise – as in the case of the *St Petersburg Times*.

These differences are important because the financial flow may travel in either direction (Figure 2.1). The charity may be the provider of funds for the news organisation or the news organisation may be the provider of funds for the charity that are then used for other purposes.

In cases of news organisations funded by owners that are charities, the purpose is generally to support types of coverage that are not readily available in other media. These typically focus on topics, issues, communities and localities that are ignored by commercial news organisations. This structural arrangement can also reduce commercial pressures on the news enterprise.

Figure 2.1

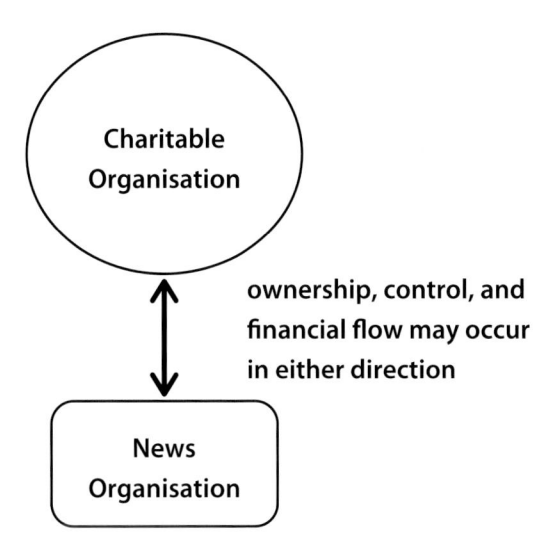

```
        ┌─────────────┐
        │  Charitable │
        │ Organisation│
        └─────────────┘
               ↕         ownership, control, and
                         financial flow may occur
                         in either direction
        ┌─────────────┐
        │    News     │
        │ Organisation│
        └─────────────┘
```

The amount of funding provided by the charitable organisation is dependent upon the financial resources of that organisation. If the charity relies upon an endowment, the level of support it provides is determined by the size of its endowment, the financial performance of its investments, and the effectiveness of its administration. In cases where the charity collects funds from donors for use by the news organisation (a means of obtaining tax benefits for donors), the level of support it provides is dependent upon its success in raising funds from donors, its costs for doing so, and the effectiveness of its management. In such arrangements the news enterprise may or may not raise additional revenue through other activities such as advertising, circulation, and other sales. Whether they engage in such activities is the result of individual choice or of operational limitations in charity laws in some countries.

Structural arrangements in which the charity is funded by a commercial news organisation are created to provide a revenue stream to support the charitable aims of the creator. In these constructions, the financial resources available to the charity are dependent on the financial performance of the news organisation, which is typically operated as a for-profit enterprise. In this situation, the charitable arrangement can actually lead to profit demands that are little different from the demands of other private owners.

Only a limited amount of research exists on foundation-owned firms of all types. One study of foundation-owned firms across German industries found higher labour intensity, lower salaries, and lower productivity in foundation-owned firms when compared to corporations (Herrmann and Franke, 2002). Others found they could be as profitable as non-foundation-owned firms and that there were some advantages related to long-term business strategy (Thomsen, 1999; Thomsen and Caspar, 2004), but that challenges arose in corporate governance, management, and finance and they were more risk adverse (Fama and Jensen, 1983; Bennett et al., 2003).

Studies on not-for-profit media are highly limited, but note they create the potential to augment local coverage (Shaver, 2010) and lessen commercial pressures, but that papers owned by charities tend to have mixed performance (Picard and Van Weezel, 2008).

This occurs because these arrangements do not guarantee resources necessary to produce high quality content, do not ensure regular reinvestment, and do not provide incentives for managers and employees to improve quality or market performance. Such arrangements also do not shield firms from underlying economic and financial forces that affect all enterprise – whether commercial or non-commercial.

Charitably supported media

Charitably supported media receive funds provided by charitable entities and individuals to support the activities of the organisations (Figure 2.2). In these arrangements the charity does not actually own or control the news organisation, but provides financing for a portion or all of its activities.

These news organisations may or may not be for-profit enterprises, but most have traditionally been not-for-profit organisations.[1] A charity may exist to support a single or several journalistic organisations or to provide funding to support particular types of journalism or journalistic practice. Individuals may also provide financial support directly to the news enterprise or they may donate to a charitable organisation as a conduit for that purpose, thus receiving tax benefits because news enterprises themselves typically are not or cannot be charitable organisations in many countries.

Figure 2.2

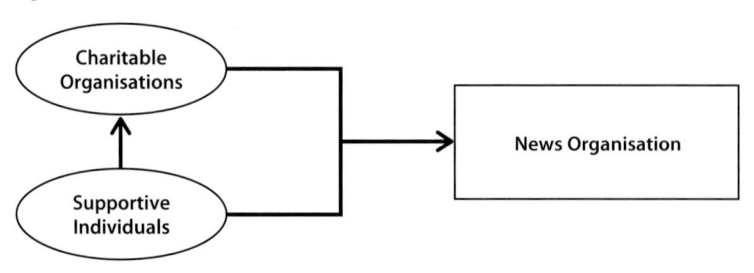

---

[1] The terms non-profit and not-for-profit are often used synonymously, but the latter indicates that profit is not the operational motive but may be sought so the organisation may reinvest surplus to help it grow and prosper. In recent years it has become a preferred term by professionally managed public service and charitable organisations.

These arrangements are illustrated in the United States by ProPublica – which won the Pulitzer Prize for Investigative Reporting in 2010 – that is funded by the Sandler Foundation and other donors and by the Knight Foundation which has been the largest supporter of start-up non-profit digital news organisations in that country. Google recently provided additional funds for the project through the Knight Foundation.

Such arrangements are typically created to support media that cover topics, issues, or localities that are uninteresting to commercial enterprises. Consequently, most charitably supported media operate as non-profit or not-for-profit firms. Studies of non-profit magazines have shown they do not grow as rapidly as for-profit magazines, that they differ widely in revenue sources and strength, and have had difficulties maintaining revenues in the past decade (Mcguire, 2009). There is significant interest on the part of foundations for assisting alternative news organisations, but a recent study warns that their support is 'primarily limited to start-ups and is unlikely to provide a long-term, sustainable revenue stream' (Shaver, 2010). Sustainability issues are compounded because news personnel who have founded or moved into management charitable non-profit enterprises report themselves ill prepared for the marketing requirements and difficulties in attracting capital needed to operate (Tyree, 2010) and are generally uninterested in the managerial tasks needed to make such firms successful and sustainable.

Trust ownership

Trust ownership or control takes place when news organisations are placed in the hands of trustees and they are obligated to operate them in certain ways. The trust may dictate business and financial dealings, may require adherence to certain standards and traditions, or may require loyalty to certain political, social, or religious viewpoints. They may or may not be created as charities and many trusts are created to avoid some tax payments, particularly inheritance taxes.

The primary rationale for journalistic trusts is to create managerial and editorial independence, so they differ significantly from the other two charitably oriented structures. Trusts may fully or partially own media organisations, but they typically have control over fundamental values and strategic choices of the enterprises with which they are associated.

Two primary distinctive types of trust ownership and control exist: one in which the trust fully owns the news enterprise (and thus controls it) and another in which the trust has some control over decisions or operations by virtue of structural arrangements with the company (Figure 2.3).

As noted earlier, many news trusts were created in the UK between the 1940s and 1960s to preserve the political leanings of papers that press barons sold to other companies. These included provisions governing the *Birmingham Post and Mail*, the *Bristol Evening Post and Evening World*, the *Daily News*, *The Economist*, the *Guardian*, the *Liverpool Daily*

Post and Echo, the *Observer*, the *Spectator*, and the *Yorkshire Post* and *Evening Post*.

Figure 2.3

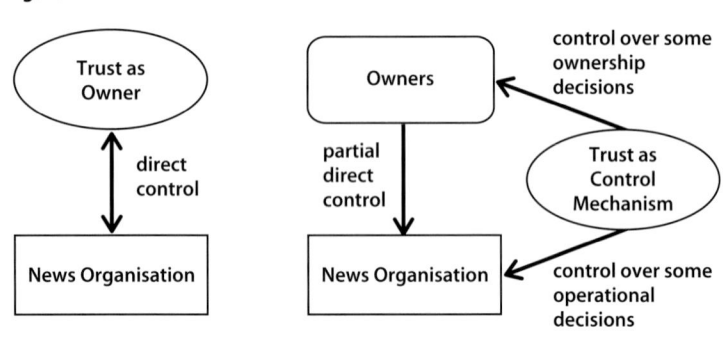

```
    Trust as                    Owners  ←── control over some
    Owner                                   ownership
                                            decisions
      ↕                           │
   direct                      partial        Trust as
   control                     direct         Control
                               control       Mechanism
      ↓                           ↓
   News Organisation          News Organisation  ←── control over some
                                                     operational
                                                     decisions
```

A look at that list immediately shows that trusts are no guarantee of survival because a number of the papers have since been shut down or merged away into other publications. The *Daily News* was never very successful commercially, merging with other papers three times between 1912 and 1930, and ultimately ceasing publication in 1960 as part of a merger with the *Daily Mail*. The *Observer* was sold to Atlantic Richfield Co. in 1977 and Lonrho in 1981 before being integrated into the Guardian Media Group in 1993. The *Spectator* is now owned by the *Daily Telegraph*.

Media trusts are found in many nations and often involve well-known news enterprises. The Schibsted Media Group that is based in Norway, for example, is under the control of the Tinius Trust. *Frankfurter Allgemeine Zeitung* – one of the most respected papers in Germany – is controlled by the FAZIT-Stiftung. *The New York Times* is controlled by a family trust that owns preferential shares in the company.

Compared to enterprises owned or supported by charities, trust-owned or controlled news organisations tend to be much larger and are typically operated as commercial enterprises.

Trusts face a number of challenges, including finding good trustees because expertise – as well as commitment to trust principles – is needed and there are limited financial incentives for most trustees since they do not own shares in the firm. Some organisations, particularly charitable trusts, face limitations on acquiring capital necessary for reinvestment and growth.

Research has shown that boards drawn from the community provide legitimacy for trust-controlled and non-profit organisations by representing different interests in the community (Abzug and Galaskiewicz, 2001). Such boards are often ineffective and need better governance and management structuring to successfully meet the challenges facing the organisations (Carver, 2006) and even board members have widely differing perspectives of their effectiveness (Herman et al., 2006).

Discussion

The various forms of charitable and trust ownership and support of media result from differences in business, charity, and tax laws in different countries, the individual histories of organisations and their founders, and strategic choices made in organisations.

It is not possible to say which is preferable or offers the most effective solution to contemporary challenges of news organisations because the opportunities to establish the various forms differ widely. Nevertheless it is possible to identify some advantages and disadvantages of the three primary structures and their substructures of such arrangements (Figure 2.4).

Overall, the primary advantages of the forms seem to result from reducing influences of commercial aspects of news business on content and improving the sustainability of news enterprises and providing means for preserving core journalistic values. The primary disadvantages seem to involve shifting dependency to non-commercial activities, potential loss of effectiveness in management of firms, and potential for conflicts with journalistic values created by the interests or views of funders and trust founders.

Although some forms reduce commercial pressures or profit demands, none of the arrangements protect against changes in media use (such declines in viewers, listeners, or readers, or decline in the amount of time devoted to use), changes in advertising expenditures made to a particular medium, or declines in revenue due to economic downturns.

The importance of governance issues to the structural forms cannot be ignored, especially in the selection and succession of trustees and boards of charitably owned or supported news enterprises. Boards often tend to be well populated with individuals with social and charity-sector backgrounds, but less so with technological, financial, and business management backgrounds. The choice of trustees and board members can deny or provide knowledge and skills needed to sustain the organisation over the long run.

Because trusts tend to put emphasis on media form and organisational stability, some trusts may be more organisationally constrained in responding to industry developments and trends. A trust with the express purpose of supporting a newspaper might be less willing to engage in digital activities or changes in its structures and operations. Some evidence of reticence is seen in *Le Monde*, over which journalists have a great deal of control, and which has a history of difficulty in responding to changing circumstances. The Scott Trust and the *Guardian's* leadership in digital media, however, opens that point to question, although we have yet to see whether they might be less willing to cease print publication as the digital future continues.

Figure 2.4

	Advantages	Disadvantages
Charitable Ownership of Media	• Reduces profit demands if charity funds media • Tendency to produce longer-term business strategy • Produces a revenue stream that can supplement consumer or advertising streams (if any) • Charity has some commitment to the survival and continued operation of news enterprise	• Support is dependent on financial resources of the charity and its fundraising abilities • News organisation may be used to provide funds for the charity, creating profit demands • Limitations of sources of capital if firms are not-for-profit operations • Philosophical, religious, political views of charity may (but do not necessarily) conflict with journalistic values • Tendency to remove incentives for growth and reinvestment
Charitably Supported Media	• Operation of the news organisation remains somewhat independent of charity • Reduces or removes reliance on commercial activities • Reduces fundraising orientation and effort within the news enterprise itself	• Funder attachment is philosophical and psychological rather than economic self interest • Tendency to dependency on charitable funding rather than developing new enterprise self funding • Tendency for short-term (or no) business strategy • Tendency to remove incentives for growth and reinvestment
(a) charitable organisations	• News organisation can concentrate efforts on journalistic activity • Individual donors receive tax benefits when funds are funnelled through charitable organisation	• Overhead costs and administrative efficiency of charitable organisations affects amount of support received • When large numbers of small donors are involved, great effort/expense to obtain and maintain support is required
(b) supportive individuals	• Support comes from individuals committed to the ideal of news organisation, but not directly controlling it • Engages readers, listeners, and viewers at a higher level and increases loyalty	• News organisation must itself be a charitable organisation so individuals may receive tax benefits from contributions if it directly receives money • Charitable status may limit abilities to take stands on political issues • When large numbers of small donors are involved, great effort/expense to obtain and maintain support is required
Trust Ownership	• Preserves character of news organisation and principles and of the trust founder • Ability to preserve adherence to journalistic and democratic values in for-profit news enterprises	• Fewer incentives for knowledgeable, engaged trustees • Limitations of sources of capital if not-for-profit enterprises are involved
(a) Trust as owner	• Tends to continue sustainability and growth demands • Tendency to produce mid-term business strategy	• Philosophical, religious, political views of charity may (but do not necessarily) conflict with journalistic values
(b) Trust as control mechanism	• Involvement of trustees in organisational control tends to be limited to ensuring principles of trust are followed	• Philosophical, religious, political views of charity may (but do not necessarily) conflict with journalistic values

Some trusts may be more organisationally constrained in responding to industry developments and trends

The choice of structures is not always determinable by those who work within the enterprise. In established firms, it may be a legacy put in place by a founder or previous owner. In these cases, the choice has already been made and the ability to alter the arrangements may be limited by terms of the arrangements or law. Existing enterprises not yet under any of the arrangements may be transformed into one of the charitable and trust ownership and control forms, depending upon the will of its owners. Organisers of start-up enterprises have the greatest leeway in determining structures because they do so at inception and are not limited by pre-existing conditions in the firm.

Many owners of existing commercial news firms typically lack incentives and willingness to alter their current structures because doing so would mean giving up profits and a significant amount of control over the enterprise. Where ownership of existing organisations are about to undergo a generational change or be altered by other factors, charitable and trust ownership and control may have some attractiveness to the existing owner by providing a measure of influence after the ownership changes. These alternative structures may also be attractive where market turbulence has damaged commercial enterprises and mechanisms and time are sought to transform and preserve them.

These alternatives may be interesting to and desirable for some small start-up news enterprises, but they will not be appropriate for all because of their limitations in terms of capitalisation, revenue, and governance. Clearly, independence from commercial interests and profit demands are attractive to many journalists and community activists considering new types of news media, but the extent to which such start-ups are able to stop worrying about financial matters and can be sustained over time is not yet clear.

Charitable and trust ownership of news enterprises thus provide some opportunities and advantages in starting new journalistic enterprises and maintaining some existing organisations. The various forms, however, all carry with them disadvantages – some quite significant – so they should not be seen as a panacea to the challenges facing legacy news organisations. Nevertheless, they may be useful mechanisms in specific individual situations and conditions and provide some succour for those wrestling with the sustainability issues facing news enterprise today.

References

Abzug, R., and Galaskiewicz (2001) 'Nonprofit Boards: Crucibles of Expertise or Symbols of Local Identities?', *Nonprofit and Voluntary Sector Quarterly*, 30(1): 51–73.

Akst, Daniel (2005) 'Nonprofit Journalism: Removing the Pressure of the Bottom Line', *Carnegie Reporter*, 3/3 (Fall); www.carnegie.org/reporter/11/nonprofjourn/index.html (accessed Jan. 2010).

Andrews, Amanda (2009) 'Guardian Staff Told to Expect Redundancies', I (16 Sept.), B2.

Bennett, J., Iossa, E., and Legrenzi, G. (2003) 'The Role of Commercial Non-Profit Organizations in the Provision of Public Services', *Oxford Review of Economic Policy*, 19: 335–47.

Carver, J. (2006) *Boards that Make a Difference: A New Design for Leadership in Nonprofit and Public Organizations*, 3rd edn (San Francisco: Jossey-Bass).

Conlan, Tara (2008) 'Guardian Owners the Scott Trust to be Wound Up After 72 Years', Guardian 8 Oct.; www.guardian.co.uk/media/2008/oct/08/theguardian.

Downey Jr., Leonard, and Schudson, Michael (2009) 'The Reconstruction of American Journalism', *Columbia Journalism Review*, 19 Oct.; www.cjr.org/reconstruction/the_reconstruction_of_american.php?page=all (accessed Jan. 2011).

Fama, E. F., and Jensen, M. C. (1983)
'Separation of Ownership and Control', *Journal of Law and Economics*, 26: 301–25.

Guardian Media Group (2008) 'Scott Trust Updates Structure', 8 Oct.; www.gmgplc.co.uk/media/pressreleases/tabid/213/default.aspx?pressreleaseid=121&cid=viewdetails.

Herman, Robert D., Renz, David O. M., and Heimovics, Richard D. (2006) 'Board Practices and Board Effectiveness in Local Nonprofit Organizations', *Nonprofit Management and Leadership*, 7(4): 373–385.

Herrmann, Markus, and Franke, Günter (2002) 'Performance and Policy of Foundationn owned Firms in Germany', *European Financial Management*, 8(3): 261–79.

Loundy, Mark (2007) 'Newspapers as Non-Profits?', *News Photographer*, 62/11 (27 Nov.), 16.

Mcguire, Miles (2009) 'The Nonprofit Business Model: Empirical Evidence from the Magazine Industry', *Journal of Media Economics*, 22(3): 119–33.

Ofcom (2009) *Local and Regional Press in the UK*, Discussion Document, 22 Sept.

Picard, Robert G., and Van Weezel, Aldo (2008) 'Capital and Control: Consequences of Different Forms of Newspaper Ownership', *International Journal on Media Management*, 10: 21–32.

Pickard, Victor, Stearns, J., and Aaron, C. (2009) *Saving the News: Toward a National Journalism Strategy* (Washington, DC: Free Press).

Political and Economic Planning (1959) 'The Work of Newspaper Trusts', *PEP Planning*, 25/435 (24 Aug.), 135–58.

Reilly Center for Media and Public Affairs (2008) *The Breaux Symposium: New Models for News* (Baton Rouge, LA: Louisiana State University).

Royal Commission (1949) *Royal Commission on the Press, 1947–1949: Report* (London: HMSO, CMd. 7700).

Schiffrin, André (2007) 'How to Pay for a Free Press', *Le Monde Diplomatique English* (Oct.); http://mondediplo.com/2007/10/13publishing (accessed Jan. 2010).

Shaver, Dan (2010) 'Online Non-Profits Provide Model for Added Local News', *Newspaper Research Journal*, 32(4): 16–28.

The Times (2008) 'Guardian Media Group Plots Closure of Observer Newspaper', 2 Aug.; http://business.timesonline.co.uk/tol/business/industry_sectors/media/article6736037.ece (accessed Jan. 2011).

Thomsen, S. (1999) 'Corporate Ownership by Industrial Foundations', *European Journal of Law and Economics*, 7: 117–37.

— and Caspar, R. (2004) 'Foundation Ownership and Financial Performance: Do Companies Need Owners?', *European Journal of Law and Economics*, 18, 343–64.

Tyree, Christopher (2010) 'Newspaper Employee to Nonprofit Director: A Photojournalist's Journey', *Nieman Reports* (Spring), 26–8.

United States, Federal Trade Commission (2010) 'Potential Policy Recommendations to Support the Reinvention of Journalism', FTC Staff Discussion Draft.

Weisberg, Jacob (2009) 'Dubious New Models for News', *Newsweek* (2 Mar.); www.newsweek.com/id/185804 (accessed Jan. 2010).

3. Regional Press Challenges Promote Calls for New Ownership Forms and Legal Bases

Neil Fowler

The UK regional newspaper industry is in crisis. It is in the jaws of an extraordinary pincer movement of structural change and economic downturn resulting in an increasing number of publications being closed and journalism jobs being lost, with potentially alarming ramifications for local democracy and the generation of news. It is the forerunner of all current media in the UK – and whether it prospers or falls could fundamentally alter the free flow of information in this country. But its influence has been, and remains, immense.

This decline, in sharp focus in 2011, has accelerated since 2007, though analysis of sales figures since the late 1960s shows that the deterioration has been in place for decades. For example, regional morning and evening sales in 1961 reached 8.7m copies a day. Fifty years later that figure, including various editions of the free Metro as well as the Evening Standard in London, was down to 4.73m. Strangely the number of publications was broadly similar, perhaps showing that there is some resilience in the brands. There were 92 dailies in 1961 compared with 89 in 2011 – a number that increases to 103 when free titles, not around in 1961, are taken into account.

However, the introduction of mass classified advertising in the early 1960s, the expansion of the UK economy from the late 1980s through to the start of the 2008 recession, and the substantial financial windfalls gained from the introduction of new technology (and the removal of the print unions) and from the sales of Reuters shares, have masked this decrease.

Structurally not much has changed over the decades. Newspapers are owned by a mixture of larger groups and smaller individual businesses, as they have been since the 1930s. The balance is more heavily weighed to the group now, but the overwhelming majority operate under standard business rules and limited company methods. Few experiments have taken place to see if any variations on these themes can be successful.

Can this structure both maintain itself and keep a regional and local press in business? There is a growing belief among some commentators that there needs to be a radical change in the ownership of such bodies if they are to survive and the conduit of local news and scrutiny is to remain.

Ofcom, in its 2009 review *Local and Regional Media in the UK*, recognised the importance of the local press to the food chain of news and expressed concern at its future. Andrew Currah, in a paper for the Reuters Institute for the Study of Journalism in the same year, put forward a series of recommendations to enable local news to be maintained if established businesses were to fail. The Joseph Rowntree Reform Trust has been supporting investigations into charitable status for local and regional newspapers. The whole issue of whither or wither the regional and local press in the UK is therefore very much in play. The time to explore possible new forms of ownership is here.

The time to explore possible new forms of ownership is here

Long-term problems

The simple view is that the internet has been the sole cause of the industry's ills. But it is a much more complex problem than that. Regional and local newspapers have faced a perfect storm of factors that have been developing over decades to bring them to their knees.

The slow process started in the 1950s when British society began moving out of its post-war gloom and economic growth took hold and gave the public more to do than read the cheap and the sometimes cheerful printed word of newspapers. The beginning of the end of the age of the regional and local newspaper as a means of mass communication to the total audience of a particular community had begun.

This sector of the newspaper industry was not particularly well equipped to adapt and evolve in line with these changes. Economically, publications were stable but slow-moving entities, often encumbered with necessarily unimaginative managers who were weighed down with dealing with the might of the print unions; politically, ownership and consolidation were subjects that were never exposed above the parapet; and sociologically there was a sense that already they were seen as yesterday's news.

The industry had grown rapidly in the nineteenth century, based on the investments of local patrician owners, who were keen to both make money and to see a voice for their home areas. Some multi-title groups developed in the early twentieth century, with some swapping of publications before the Second World War being early examples of consolidation.

In the post-war period many major provincial cities still maintained two evening newspapers. This competitive state had largely disappeared by the end of the 1960s. What two-title markets remained were generally in the form of a morning-evening duopoly, published by the same organisation.

There were occasional changes in ownership style to maintain the founding principles of certain newspapers, though their basic business activities remained the same.

In 1935 a complicated share structure backed up by a deed of trust was established by the Bristol United Press Ltd which was aimed at ensuring the independence of the *Bristol Evening Post* under its own board of management and that it would continue to be of service to the Bristol public. In 1944 a similar deed was drawn up to ensure the *Birmingham Post and Evening Mail* maintained for twenty-one years their local and independent nature, free from control by any political party, trade association, or London newspaper. But, apart from these two examples, the basic composition of the sector didn't change.

From 1945 to the early 1980s the industry trundled along. Profits were solid but not spectacular. Innovation was rare, despite the introduction of bulk classified advertising from North America by Roy Thomson in the 1960s and the attempt to ring London by Thomson and Westminster Press with a circle of suburban evenings.

The economy was changing. Industrialisation was in decline and the factories outside which regional daily newspapers had sold hundreds of thousands of copies every day were shutting. The growth of driving to and from work, rather than by walking or by bus, exacerbated this effect.

The print unions were feared by managements, which had little success in combating them. Three Royal Commissions on the Press did little to stimulate the regional sector, merely commenting on the inexpensiveness of the UK's system of distributing news. Sales were generally (with some notable exceptions) in gentle decline from the late 1960s. Newspaper paginations were small with smaller selling evening publications often producing just 10-page broadsheet or 20-page tabloid editions.

Free newspapers were introduced in to the UK in the mid-1960s, generally by local small-scale entrepreneurs looking to challenge the established order. But even this new concept didn't spark too many worries. Traditional owners launched their own spoilers against the upstarts and hoped they would go away. Some did, others, like Lionel Pickering and Keith Barwell, did not and became multi-millionaires when they sold out to bigger groups a couple of decades later.

The golden years

Then came the quiet rout of the print unions on the back of regional industrial confrontations, initially at Nottingham in 1973, followed by Wolverhampton and Portsmouth in the early 1980s, and then the

Warrington dispute in 1983 that helped to inspire News International to move its national titles to Wapping without its traditional print work force in 1986. Most regional businesses, notably the big groups which had been happy to watch smaller, independent organisations in places such as Nottingham and Wolverhampton take the risks, subsequently carried out their own reorganisations without any of the attendant confrontation.

The industry then enjoyed its golden years and was able to invest properly in capital equipment. Much of the initial investment in the new computers was funded by the goldmine created by the 1984 flotation of Reuters, owned in part since 1941 by many different UK national, regional, and local newspapers (through their memberships of both the Newspaper Publishers Association and their ownership of the Press Association), along with some Commonwealth press agencies. Reuters suddenly and unexpectedly began producing both profits and dividends and the opportunity was taken to exploit this newfound value.

Most of the industry had shed its compositors by the early 1990s and profits, assisted by a developing economy, advanced rapidly. Newspaper paginations increased substantially, the days of 10-page broadsheet editions went and more journalists were recruited to fill the demanding hunger of the expanding news hole. The style of newspaper changed, too. Some regional dailies tried to ape their national tabloid cousins, and overall there was an increase in the use of human interest lifestyle reporting and information provision, the so-called 'news you can use'.

New titles were launched: Thomson introduced three Sunday publications for the nations – *Scotland on Sunday, Wales on Sunday*, and *Sunday Life* in Northern Ireland. Thomson also launched an evening title for a city that had never had such a publication – *Chester Tonight*. There were moments of joy when newspapers sale spiked, generally on the back of relaunches from broadsheet to tabloid, but sales still maintained their slow decline and businesses did not seem to be too concerned as recruitment advertising, in particular, funded substantial returns.

At the start of 2007 there was the perception that all was rosy. The Newspaper Society, the representative organisation of the regional press, said that the industry still accounted for 16.1% of all UK advertising spend – behind the internet (16.5%) and television (23.1%); and that more than 40m of the country's population saw a regional paper at least once a week. The sector employed more than 40,000 people, including 12,000 journalists.

A growth in consolidation

There had been a growth in consolidation. In the previous twelve years four of the five major groups of the 1990s – Thomson Regional Newspapers, Westminster Press, United Provincial Newspapers, and Reed Regional Newspapers – had largely disappeared to be replaced by the groups that had acquired and merged in an aggressive fashion – Trinity Mirror, Johnston Press, and Newsquest (owned by the USA's Gannett). The only constant major group was Northcliffe Newspapers, owned by the Daily Mail and General Trust (DMGT) which was largely in the same form (with some additions and subtractions) that had been developed by the first Lord Rothermere before 1939.

By then these four groups were responsible for some 75% of the market, including daily, weekly, paid-for, and free publications (including the daily free *Metro* and the London *Evening Standard*). Three other groups – Archant, Iliffe, and Tindle Newspapers – all published at least forty titles each and there were substantial local businesses that had very strong micro presences, such as the CN Group in Cumbria, the Kent Messenger group in Kent, and the Midland News Association in Wolverhampton and Shropshire.

Overall there were ninety-one separate groups publishing slightly more than 1,300 titles, turning over nearly £4bn producing an estimated £848m operating profit. The top twenty groups were responsible for around 97% of total circulation and distribution and 85% of all titles.

At that time shares of the two principal publicly quoted regional businesses, Johnston Press and Trinity Mirror, were holding up well, targeting 30% margins from their constituent businesses; acquiring debt to fund further purchase of other newspaper businesses was not seen as a problem. The City enjoyed the 30% margins too and seemed to believe the rhetoric that they would carry on for many years in the future.

But in 2008 the industry began to suffer some palpitations. Share prices of Johnston and Trinity Mirror began to fall steeply and have barely recovered since.

What was then the country's longest established major regional newspaper group, Northcliffe, had been placed on the market by its owners in 2007 – but a buyer could not be found – or rather DMGT declined an offer of £1.1bn, a decision it began to regret just a few months later.

Although some consolidation had taken place over the years, wholesale amalgamation was restricted by regulation, which meant that already there were examples of newspapers, including one of the UK's first free weekly newspapers, the *Derby Trader*, which could have been saved by a takeover but which had been closed.

The loss of classified

The regionals' staple diet of the classified advertising categories of motoring, property and jobs, which had been developed in the early 1960s, was haemorrhaging to the internet where advertising revenue quadrupled between 2004 and 2009. Sites such as Craigslist, which had wreaked mayhem on North American newspapers, began forays into the UK. But even where they were not as successful as on the other site of the Atlantic, others such as eBay and Gumtree came in to fragment the market successfully.

In addition, retail advertising was diminishing even before the bank crisis-inspired recession struck and readership was getting older while not being replaced by any inroads into younger demographics.

However, at the same time businesses were continuing to make the 30% margins, some of the most envied in business as a whole. These though began to decline rapidly from 2007 onwards.

Regional daily newspapers (including the free *Metro* and London *Evening Standard*) were still selling and distributing some 5m copies every day. And there were still 8m Sunday and weekly paid-for newspapers sold and more than 24m free newspapers distributed every week.

At the end of 2008, the outlook seemed bleak. Analyst Claire Enders predicted that a third of the UK's regional newspapers and half of the jobs in the regional media would disappear in the next five years. She said that by 2013 she would expect the local press to have declined very substantially, saying that more than a third of regional publications would go out of business.

But two years after that prediction, although the industry had gone through a major downturn, with some titles closing and jobs lost, the perceived general structural picture at the beginning of 2011 had not changed that much.

The position in 2011

At the start of 2011, the top twenty regional press publishers accounted for 87% of all regional press titles and 97% of total weekly circulation, about the same as 2007. There were eighty-seven regional press publishers producing a total of 1,196 titles. This included thirty-nine publishers producing just one title. In 2009 there were 1,290 titles, so ninety-four had been lost over the year, but of those four were regionalised daily editions of the free Metro, seventeen were weekly paid-fors and the overwhelming majority, seventy-three, were free titles. The majority of the closed publications were positioned two or three in their market places so no area was bereft of coverage. No daily titles were lost, with a net reduction of four publishers, all of which owned one title. There remained ninety-three paid-for daily titles.

The major groups were still Trinity Mirror, Johnston Press, Newsquest, and Northcliffe and they accounted for 66% of titles and about 70% of total sales after the London *Evening Standard* had been sold by DMGT to Russian Alexander Lebedev.

The intermediate businesses were still largely the same, too, with Tindle Newspapers, Iliffe Media, DC Thomson, the Kent Messenger Group, the CN Group in Cumbria, and Midland News Association being the main players. These businesses had reduced paginations and staff since 2007 but, where they had no debt, they were seen to be surviving relatively successfully.

Although the smallest sixty-seven publishers accounted for just 3% of total circulation and distribution they were responsible for 13% of titles. These publishers included many family firms, focusing on tight geographical areas, and the country's only charitable trust-owned newspaper, *The Maidenhead Advertiser*.

But that was the good news. Circulation declines were having a marked effect on usage. In 2009 TGI (Target Group Index) data showed that 80.4% of all adults read a regional newspaper at least once a week. A year later this figure had declined to 75.6% – a major fall, but still a healthy penetration. It might be falling, but there still seemed to remain a fundamental and substantial public appetite for local news.

However, underneath the perceived structure, many changes had taken place. The sector's share of the advertising revenue was continuing to decline. Total spending fell from £3.13bn in 2004 to £1.71bn in 2009. Market share also fell substantially, too. In 2004 the regional press took 20% of the UK's advertising spend; by 2009 the share had declined to 11.6%. The internet's share had grown from 4% to 24% and had taken percentages from every other advertising sector with the exception of cinema. The other two print sectors, magazines and national press, also declined markedly.

Circulation was being reduced at an industry average of 5% per annum but aggressive cover price increases had helped to soften circulation revenue losses. All companies, especially the major groups, took part in long-running cost-cutting programmes through making the most of improved communications technology. Many presses were closed and evening publications were printed overnight, often in remote group print centres. Editions were cut, back offices were merged, sales teams were outsourced, and paginations were reduced.

Aggressive cover price increases had helped to soften circulation revenue losses

Daily and weekly editorial teams were merged and in morning/evening centres joint staffs producing material for both titles were created. District offices were closed, pay freezes were imposed, and, in groups, companies were merged under a smaller layer of senior management.

This meant that in 2010 the major groups were able to report either a return to profitability or an increase in earnings. However Johnston Press, in particular, and Trinity Mirror, to a certain extent, were held back by the serious debt they had both developed over the previous years in expanding and this acted as a drag on their share prices.

But it wasn't all doom and gloom. Ray Tindle, proprietor of Tindle Newspapers, was bullish in a speech to a conference in May 2010:

> *Our profits for the two years of this dreadful recession are as near as dammit the same as those of the normal pre-boom times of a decade ago. We were happy then and we are not unhappy now with both sets of figures.*
>
> *... I can tell you that the recession year 2009/10 just ended at March 31 and the recession year before that 2008/9 – taken together had profits over half of the boom years of 2006/7 and 2007/8. So with recession results roughly equal to normal years before the boom and over half the boom profits, and with the recession now hopefully fading and revenue rising again, and Ernst & Young having just forecast strong growth next year – 2011.*

After a hesitant start to how the sector should approach the internet, all newspapers had worked out their web policies, drawn up their rate cards, and were writing in real time for their sites. Some experiments had been tried, paywalls of various kinds had been trialled but there was little consistency across the sector. Some were completely open, some offered limited access until after publication of their print titles, others sold online page-turning paid-for editions, but there was no consensus on what was the optimum model.

Changing content

How newspapers covered their patches had clearly been affected by the reduction in staff numbers. There was growing concern that local government in particular and some courts, too, were beginning to lack scrutiny by regional and local newspapers, so producing a democratic deficit whereby county and district councils in England, for example, could operate without any outside input. However, in a report by this author to the Press Association in 2009, this effect was found to be patchy (Fowler, 2009).

Broadly daily editors whose newspapers covered larger urban areas believed they were doing a good job when there was just one or two councils to cover, while the coverage of authorities which were outside those areas was diminishing.

Multi-title centres that had retained some district offices were still able to scrutinise to a reasonable level of effectiveness. Ironically the introduction of single-tier local authorities had assisted this. City dailies, where a unitary authority now exists, could still cover those authorities with a lot of detail. Larger centres, which had retained bigger staffs, were able to invest more hours in to local government and courts reporting.

Smaller daily titles and weeklies were having more problems. A council is a council, whatever sized newspaper covers it, and so small papers need to invest relatively more time to cover them. Areas where two-tier government still existed had the main issues. The county council was losing out and major policy issues of county-wide importance (social services and education are the main county-level responsibilities) were going unreported and failing to be examined for communities covered by such newspapers.

The report found that some weekly publications were relying too much on council press offices, merely reproducing their release verbatim, and experience of local government reporting was being lost. As older staff left, they were not being replaced with those who saw the value in both career and financial terms of such a role in the long term. Knowledge of how local government works was lacking and trainees were not being equipped with the correct skills.

For some weekly titles this was not a problem. For generations they had existed on being genuinely local and could concentrate on their core area as they had always done so. But many daily papers in particular found themselves in a vicious downward spiral. Advertising revenue was in freefall, circulation revenue was slipping as sales fell despite more assertive pricing policies, which resulted in the need to cut more costs. This meant that editions and district offices were further reduced, the coverage of outlying areas declined, councils and courts went unreported; there was less reason to purchase and read the paper if you lived outside the core area.

Stark dilemmas

There were some stark dilemmas at the start of 2011. Advertising revenue had declined but was still sizeable with a slow but noticeable increase in online income. Higher yielding classified had disappeared (as much a problem for the serious end of the national newspaper market), online recruitment had dipped for the time being, and there were fewer display advertisers.

Shares in the two public limited companies highly dependent on regional publications were not viewed that favourably by the City; Johnston Press was very low, while Trinity Mirror had risen slightly on the back of rumours of a merger with another European regional publisher but was still depressed. The third publicly traded UK company which had interests in the regional sector, the Daily Mail and General Trust, was performing well on the back of a massively changed and diversified business helped by its Northcliffe Newspapers division playing an increasingly less significant role in the total profile of the business.

Profits were down but appeared to be steadying. Gannet claimed that its Newsquest division was still highly profitable and Johnston reported that in the first half of 2010 it had increased its operating profit for the first time in four years. Its margin was 19.5% for the period, though there was an acceptance that the 30% margins were no longer sustainable, with Trinity Mirror now asking for 10%. Circulation of the daily market continued to be down but there were signals that the rate of decrease was slowing. Weeklies whose sales had been generally resilient were now affected but many titles still sold significant numbers.

Costs, which were always closely monitored in the regions, have been heavily reduced even more as many functions were centralised as technology allowed and others outsourced. Printing press sites have been reduced enormously and the remaining centres are worked 24 hours day. There is no issue with one group printing another's titles. Johnston Press's accounting and financial services for all its centres are now handled from one office in Peterborough. The same happens for Northcliffe on one floor of its Leicester office. Most evening newspapers are now printed overnight, with few having an on-the-day edition, though they are not produced as true morning titles.

Cover prices had been neglected since the war, the belief being that they were too price inelastic to be increased too rapidly. But more aggression had allowed this revenue to play a more significant role in businesses.

Models for the future

However, the sign for the future in 2010 was the sales performances of the twenty-two daily paid-for newspapers owned by businesses outside the big four – generally family or non-traded companies. For the first half of 2010, fifteen of these twenty-two were in the top twenty-four of best performing year-on-year circulation figures. Conversely this meant that only eight out of seventy-one owned by the big four were in the same top twenty-four. All but one of these sales performances were down, but there was a clear relationship between the type of ownership and achievement.

And most newspapers have a long way to go before they are unviable. Jim Chisholm's 2009 report showed that for many regional companies the main problem was debt, not profitability, and that they had expanded by buying other businesses that were declining, rather than investing in ways of reversing long-established falling sales trends. He argued that they could develop other revenue streams in linked marketing activities and not just depend on an advertising sector of a rapidly changing overall marketing expenditure.

Most newspapers have a long way to go before they are unviable

Currently in the UK there are the numerous business models. The big four dominate, but groups have thrived for many decades. In the 1960s and 1970s Thomson, Westminster Press, United Provincial Newspapers, Reed Regional Newspapers, and Northcliffe were the leaders, but indebtedness has brought problems to the current major players.

Underneath them lies a whole range of different styles of company, which despite falling advertising revenues may well be placed to not only survive but also potentially prosper. Privately owned Archant owns four daily newspapers in East Anglia but has expanded into consumer and country magazines. It has low debt and good cash flow. The Tindle group owns 200 small weekly titles and has no debt. The family-owned Midland News Association owns the *Express and Star* in Wolverhampton, the UK's biggest-selling evening publication, and maintains eight on-the-day editions. None of these companies have the need to satisfy City-based pension funds and other shareholders. Clearly they need profit to survive and all have made tough decisions on costs but their needs for such high margins, especially when their debt levels are low, is negated.

But it is at what is deemed the lower end of the market that the existing model changes significantly. Here 20% of all weekly paid-for newspapers are owned by publishers who account for just 1% of total combined regional and local newspaper weekly circulation. Some thirty-eight companies own just one paid-for weekly title, often, but not always, accompanied by a free supporting publication. They are low cost but with high story counts often producing significant penetrations in their local populations. They also tend to have considerable links with their communities.

In a report for the Joseph Rowntree Reform Trust in 2010 three weekly newspapers were analysed. The *Barnsley Chronicle*, which is family-owned with a sister free, the *Maidenhead Advertiser*, which as noted is the UK's only trust-owned local weekly, and the *Ashbourne News Telegraph*, owned by the private Iliffe News and Media, all displayed these characteristics.

The *Barnsley Chronicle* is a broadsheet with tabloid supplements, 39,000 paid circulation a week with a cover price of 60p, seven editions, reaching 52% of adults, and 75% with a sister free newspaper. It has some sister magazines, its own associated printing company, no significant debts, and no substantial direct competition apart from the nearby daily *Sheffield Star*, local radio, and some local bloggers, though none significant.

The tabloid *Maidenhead Advertiser* is owned and managed by the Baylis Trust, sells 22,000 a week with a cover price of 55p. It has sister editions in Windsor, Slough, Ascot and Twyford but reaches 80% of all adults within Maidenhead. It is printed on contract, has no significant debts, and its profits are distributed to local good causes. It has no significant local direct competition.

The *Ashbourne News Telegraph* in Derbyshire is a tabloid, selling about 6,250 a week at 55p and reaching 80% of all local adults. It has some daily competition from the Derby Evening Telegraph but little else.

All concentrated on local news and sport, with high numbers of pictures of local people and a strong emphasis of human interest reports. All devoted substantial coverage to local government, crime (and fires and accidents, etc.), and courts were prominent, though there were many reports of straightforward information and of everyday events that had happened. Many of these were village paragraphs and contributed to the overall high story counts.

All maintained reasonable levels of property and motoring advertising with strong paid-for obituary columns. Local service advertising, of the kind that would be lost or difficult to find on the internet, was strong, too.

Readers' input was important. All dedicated considerable amounts of space to letters and all saw nostalgia as essential, offering at least one tabloid page equivalent each week. All had local correspondents filing numerous village reports. All had websites that were serviceable rather than sparkling but fulfilled their purpose and were updated with breaking news when necessary.

These three are good examples of how there is a basis for the sector to maintain a presence in its traditional form while developing new methods of delivery through the internet and related processes. Along with the other smaller businesses they could be the foundation for the future – no debt, a recognised circulation area, a focus on very local news, names and places, and tight cost control. Alongside this kind of organisation is the hyperlocal print product, full of very localised advertising, and often emanating from small local publishers – examples of genuine under-the-radar grass-roots businesses.

The questions that need to be answered

There are some basic questions for regional and local news organisations as they face the future. Is there a demand for local and regional news? What do readers actually want? If there is, how will it be owned, structured and funded? How will consumers receive their news? Will readers pay for it? Or can news producers provide enough readers to gain sufficient response for advertisers? Will advertisers continue to look elsewhere? Who will the industry employ in providing this news? And in what numbers? What role will local bloggers and personal websites have?

For democracy there are genuine fears of a deficit as no one is left to report on councils, courts, and the police, let alone to scrutinise them. What will happen to the news flow that originates at local level and ends up in national newspapers and on the broadcast media?

There are genuine fears of a deficit as no one is left to report on councils, courts and the police, let alone to scrutinise them

Underneath all these questions lies a more basic conundrum – can the business of news gathering bring in more money than it costs to produce? It does not matter whether the news gatherer is a one-person freelance outfit or a multinational plc, the required answer is the same.

In the UK the sources of revenue have been evaporating for many years. High yielding jobs classified advertising has disappeared from print (as much a problem for the quality nationals as it is for regional titles) and is only slowly being replaced with much lower value online equivalents. Motoring (where yields have been lower since the introduction of free and specialist car magazines such as *Autotrader*) and property (where rates have been almost at cost for many newspapers following the threat by estate agents to pull out and publish their own co-operatively owned publications in the late 1980s and early 1990s) categories have stabilised to a certain extent but will never replace what has been lost in jobs.

Local display advertising has been more settled but in the period of austerity that the UK was situated in 2011 indicated that the downward pressure would be maintained.

There is a layer of advertising that remains to be exploited. Across the country there are many small, very local, glossy magazines being launched, often super parish magazines, but full of advertisements from businesses that just wish to target closely defined communities. These advertisers are too small for the internet, the search engine algorithms favouring the mass market directory style of aggregators (Yell, etc.) so they are difficult to find. They are opportunities for existing publishers to utilise if they can find models that offer good returns for these smaller businesses.

The big four are experimenting with hyperlocal websites but they are in their early days and there is no evidence that they can support a professional team of journalists, even in the background.

The other source of income is circulation revenue. Publishers have tended to be more aggressive over cover prices in the last five years. This has added to circulation declines but has meant that the imbalance between the two principal sources of income has been levelled slightly, although generally only amongst older readers. Younger consumers of news have been brought up with a different model. If they are interested in news they see it as free, either through newspapers such as *Metro*, or passed on by friends via Facebook. Their desire to pay for access to a service that they understand to be unrestricted is absent and all evidence so far indicates that they are unlikely to accept any change in the right to view what they perceive as free.

Existing publishers are trying all kinds of new-age methods. They all have websites of varying quality, they sell advertising, and attempt to monetise their links with search engines, but they mostly give away their news for free. Blogs, tweets, hyperlocal sites, and reader-generated content are all used and encouraged – but none brings in much revenue.

Can the future be of a more charitable nature?

Despite the massive problems of revenue generation, regional and local businesses can approach this new era with opportunity on their side. They have esteemed brands, often invested with massive local loyalty and of great embedded value. This is why new forms of ownership should be examined if the existing versions cannot work in the medium and long term. In the UK the overwhelming majority of newspapers are structured traditionally with shareholders (institutional or family) seeking some return on their investment or ownership.

Clearly major plcs such as Johnston Press and Trinity Mirror are doing all they can to stem the flow of declining revenues, to steady the weight of their debt issues, and to maintain readership across both print and electronic platforms in order to retain a presence in their communities. If they cannot, either voluntary or forced break-ups may happen which could result in opportunities for local individuals or groups to step in.

Most regional newspaper businesses have gone through huge stresses in cost reduction exercises to get where they are. Certainly all the smaller businesses outside the big four will have suffered from the dramatic fall in advertising revenues in recent years. But clearly some are better placed than others to stabilise and develop. In 2009/10 Archant had a turnover approximately 30% of that of Johnston Press – yet its total debt was just 5% of Johnston's and its debt management costs were correspondingly lower. This gives it a substantial advantage to consolidate and grow again.

The one traditional regional newspaper that is run by a trust with purely charitable aims is the *Maidenhead Advertiser* that has been owned and managed by the Baylis Trust since 1962. The trust was given ownership of the newspaper with the requirement for newspaper profits to be used to distribute charitable grants to local good causes. By 2009 a total endowment of nearly £12m had been established with annual total grants of around £500,000 regularly being achieved. The evidence is that local readers buying their local paper appreciate that some of what they spend will be recycled back into their community. The *Maidenhead Advertiser* is having similar advertising issues as the rest of the industry, but its charitable status gives it an excellent image story to present to its readers and its wider community.

Newspapers like the *Barnsley Chronicle*, managed by what might be termed old-fashioned patrician owners – in this case the Hewitt family – are in strong positions too. They are part of their community and have earned customer loyalty. The *Wolverhampton Express and Star* and its sister title the *Shropshire Star* are big daily newspapers, still with advertising issues, but with owners who are seen to be part of the community. The Tindle group is more widespread but its constituent newspapers make no attempt to be anything but very local. Their year-on-year circulation performances tend to reflect this.

The current coalition government has said it recognises the difficulties the regional and local press is facing and that it intends to change ownership regulations to make it easier for groups to buy, sell, and swap titles to enable some greater geographical grouping, but these changes will not produce many more savings – most of those have been made already.

Outside the regional sector there are other models of business operation. The Scott Trust (which will be explored in greater depth as a case study later in this publication), is the owner of the *Guardian* and a limited company with trustees who are the technical shareholders. It does not have charity as its core aim, that being the continuance of the *Guardian* itself, though it does have a charitable arm. But it also has a half share in the Autotrader stable (the other half having been sold for £675m in 2007) and in other magazines and radio, the profits from which go towards supporting the *Guardian*.

In Europe some non-traditional models have been developed. Regional title *Ouest-France* (another case study later in this book) became not-for profit in 1990 with all its surpluses being invested back in to the company. Its forty-four editions and near 800,000 sales make it the best read French-language newspaper in the world. It has a trustee structure of sixty-two members, but because it has no share capital, this can lead to problems of borrowing, so a complex third-party arrangement is in place to allow it to be treated more normally by the banking sector.

In Ireland, the Irish Times Trust was established in 1974 as a company limited by guarantee to ensure that *The Irish Times* would be published as an independent newspaper 'concerned with serious issues for the benefit of the community throughout the whole of Ireland free from any form of personal or of party political, commercial, religious or other sectional control'. It has no beneficial shareholders (its former owner gave up his rights in return for a 'substantial' payment), cannot pay dividends, and any profits made must be used to strengthen the newspaper. But it is not a charity, nor does it have charitable status. Its eleven trustees are required to be 'representative broadly of the community throughout the whole of Ireland', but they play no part in the day-to-day management of the company.

Internationally, organisations such as Torstar, owner of the *Toronto Star*, and Thomson Reuters are governed by founding liberal principles, yet still have a strong profit motive driving all their activities. Similarly the Poynter Institute, one of the world's leading schools of journalism, requires the *St Petersburg Times*, which it was bequeathed, to be efficient and effective in all that it does, though like Torstar and Thomson Reuters, it does have guiding founding principles too.

There is also a model in the United States based on philanthropy. The Investigative Reporting Workshop at American University in Washington, DC, was established to produce in-depth reports and inquiries for news organisations that no longer have the ability or resource to carry out such tasks. It has strong ethical rules that govern how it functions, but seeks donations from third parties to fund its operations. This is a possible solution for some businesses in countries where there is a strong tradition of giving, such as the USA, but in the UK it might not be so feasible. Certainly the current coalition government will endeavour to create such an environment but there will be many competing sectors for such funding.

UK charities law and its relevance to newspaper ownership

All these challenges and business factors facing the regional and local press bring in to play a new style of ownership that could bring tax and image advantages and develop more cohesion with a local audience – that of a charity. At a time when there have been significant declines in the level of trust in both private and public institutions, the idea and representation of charity and the third sector have remained relatively unsullied. Regional and local newspapers have a residue of trust from existing, lapsed, and non-readers that could be exploited with that considerable goodwill vested in the concept of charitable status.

Leading charity lawyer, Lord Phillips of Sudbury, has been working to establish agreement with the Charities Commission that charitable status could be granted to regional and local newspapers. In a letter to the Charity Commission in 2009 he said that he believed a local newspaper could be owned and run by a charity. He argued that it directly fitted into the provisions of clause 2(2)(e) of the Charities Act 2006 by being a principal tool for 'the advancement of citizenship or community development' within its catchment area.

He said that, given the extensive mass of information about local affairs in many local newspapers, they also directly and/or indirectly respond to other subsections in that clause such as 'the advancement of the arts, culture, heritage', 'the advancement of amateur sport', 'the advancement of environmental protection', 'the advancement of religion', and 'the advancement of education'.

He further told the Commission that section 2(3)(c)(ii) of the 2006 Act detailed the 'advancement of citizenship' and included 'the provision of civic responsibility, volunteering, the voluntary sector' – all aspects of local newspaper life that were relevant to his argument:

> *Manifestly, community development, cohesion and effectiveness are intimately and indispensably sustained by what one might call a traditional local newspaper. That is . . . one which purveys and stimulates news, information and comment about the whole life of the community served.*

Other examples, he said, were the court reports which local newspapers carried, and therefore helped to sustain law and order and to educate the public concerning crime in general. He said that the matter of charitable status was very much a live one because of the rapidly mounting problems of the sector. If the Commission were to clear the way for charitable status, that availability might aid the survival of an individual local paper or a chain of papers which might be reborn as charitable entities as an alternative to closure.

And he supported his argument with two common law court cases from Canada which would have bearing in the UK. In *Vancouver Regional FreeNet Association v Minister of National Revenue*, the plaintiff was offering a free public internet service and wished to gain charitable status, which was being opposed by the authorities. The lead judgement by the Canadian appeal court judge referred in its second paragraph to the idea of a newspaper seeking charitable status and implied that that would be possible so long as 'it controls the messages to ensure that they are consistent with a charitable purpose and are not used for some other purpose'.

The second case of interest, Lord Phillips noted, was the dissenting judgement reference to another Canadian case, *Native Communications Society*, which, on appeal, the court allowed to have charitable status. One of its main purposes was indeed the publication of a non-profit newspaper, *Kahtou*. Part of the decision was based upon the fact that the court thought that it would be educational as well as informative in providing content about culture, language and so on which would 'instil a degree of pride of ancestry in the readers' of *Kahtou* . . . thereby promoting a measure of cohesion among the Indian people of British Columbia that might otherwise be missing'.

Charitable ownership of media is not completely unknown in the UK and there already exist in the United Kingdom two examples of charities owning significant publications. The Baylis Trust, founded in 1962 to provide charitable donations to organisations mainly in the Maidenhead, Berkshire area, was granted the ownership in perpetuity of the *Maidenhead Advertiser* through its subsidiary trading arm, now called Baylis Media. Similarly Which?, the charity formerly known as Consumers' Association, owns and publishes through its trading arm Which? Ltd, the consumer campaigning magazine *Which?* Both are discussed in more detail in this book. Therefore models exist, though not in the technically and legally pure form of the charity being the newspaper/magazine and vice versa. But in the eyes of their publics these two examples are charities.

Similarly many charities, and particularly larger ones, already have what are effectively newspapers for their members, and sometimes for the wider community. Many churches publish parish magazines, which are a form of newspaper, as do many colleges and schools. These publications attract advertising in exactly the same way as newspapers do now.

And while the Charity Commission is wary of political edge, it is very much aware of the public benefit notion contained in the 2006 Act and is keen to allow the right kind of businesses to set up, providing they follow the guidelines and have adequate governing documents and are happy to be transparent and accountable. But to date no organisations have come forward meeting those requirements to the satisfaction of the Commission.

The benefits available

There are substantial benefits that would be available to a newspaper business that had gained charitable status, or those seeking to change their status:

- Newspaper groups that sold on manageable terms to a charity, established for the purpose of taking over a local paper as an alternative to simply closing everything down, could avoid incurring redundancy and other closure costs.

- These groups could also avoid illwill which could affect neighbouring publications they might wish to safeguard.

- A local paper run and owned by local people could enjoy substantial community support.

- It could be campaigning, as long as it didn't adopt a party-political or predictable stance, and this would prevent it from being bland or muted.

- Ownership of this kind gives the prospect of attracting supporting grants from local businesses and charitable foundations.

- There are many potential tax benefits through favourable relief from Corporation Tax, VAT and business rates. Surpluses, or profits, would be reinvested back into the publication and its associated website, or distributed to the community.

- Funds could be raised funds from individual citizens on a donation basis.

- Local readers could join the charity via a subscription model. All Which? subscribers, for example, have the option of becoming 'ordinary' members, who are the designated owners of the charity. They vote in trustee/council elections and have the opportunity for a say in the running of the charity. On a local basis, this influence by such 'shareholders' could be greater than that enjoyed by a national body.

- Such members could be encouraged to involve themselves in a more substantial way through volunteering in some way – writing, distributing, or selling.

- Gifts to a charity have the advantage of Gift Aid relief, a simple process in the UK. And charitable status would serve as an attraction for bequests and legacies.

- Trustees and non-executive directors would be both local people and voluntary, as trustees for charities cannot be paid by law. Despite the lack of remuneration, such roles should attract talented and enthusiastic candidates as a community newspaper would be a very visible sign of community leadership and cohesiveness. But they would have to remain objective and resist the temptation to interfere and influence editorially. Protection for the editor's independence would need to be enshrined in any founding articles of association.

- A move of this kind, provided it is supported by the correct balance of editorial, could revitalise a local paper and provide a safeguard of its community-mindedness and effectiveness.

These benefits are of value, but it is important that the sometimes restricting nature of charity laws does not limit the role a charitably based newspaper could have.

A charity newspaper would need to draw up a strong set of guiding principles that it would adhere to and that its readership would understand. It could not be politically partisan editorially and would have to serve its charitable purpose impartially, but that would not prevent it from coming down on one side or the other of contemporaneous local issues, if it did that without prejudice and based on the public need. The editorial policy would need to be even-handed in allowing access to its columns, though this would not prevent it operating necessary editorial decisions in terms of available space set against competing stories and contributions. It would have to prove that it could satisfy the necessary requirements, such as control over content, so as not to become the agent of, or voice for, any party, group, or other interest.

A charity newspaper would need to draw up a strong set of principles that it would adhere to and that its readership would understand

But that would not prevent the newspaper commenting on anything editorially, nor would it stand in the way of vigorous print and online readers' letters/comment/feedback sections, for example, which can be powerful forces within a community of sustaining and enlivening citizen engagement.

Nor should the presence in the newspaper of paid-for advertising be considered as infringing on its charitable nature, providing the key editorial tests are met. It is commonplace to find such advertisements across a plethora of charitable publications such as parish magazines, theatre programmes, charity newsletters, and so on. They do not hive off the commercial business into a separate entity and it would be unnecessary in the case of a charitable newspaper. That would simply add to the bureaucracy/expense with no apparent benefit.

Although any such newspaper would operate under the guidance of the Press Complaints Commission and the Code of Conduct as laid down by the editors' code committee, there might need to be some form of ombudsman, to ensure its political independence. A local independent person or group would be charged with responsibility for oversight of content and balance and the upholding of the founding principles and to whom complaints in the first place might be directed.

The drawbacks

The ambition would always be to employ professional staff, both editorially and sales, but there would have to be safeguards established over the balance and requirements of these staff in comparison with what was required of volunteers. But this is an issue that many other charities have to deal with on a regular basis so precedents are available.

Adhering to the disciplines of the governing document would be challenging, especially if major local political issues arose. And would a newspaper not driven by profit fail to chase, question, and test its local council and MPs, for example? Would it become lazy?

Obtaining charitable status can be a long process. Ideally a charity would already be in place to take over from a failing business but the timings may prove difficult. This may mean establishing a completely voluntary community newspaper that may become a vehicle for the longer term goal. And in this case rival publications might object to a new competitor gaining financial advantage from charitable status.

The building blocks are in place for charity law to have a significant bearing on the future of local newspapers in the UK. The success that some very local and specific charities enjoy is an indication that newspapers could gain considerable help but it still remains to be seen if those benefits will outweigh the many costs being currently suffered.

The Charity Commission has given a cautious welcome to Lord Phillips's arguments but it wants to see a live application to test its reservations. Its concerns focus on the strength of the governing documents and how they can prove that what the newspaper plans to do is for the public benefit, what the ethics and standards are that the newspaper will adhere to, and the decisions that go in to determining what organisations would be held to account by the newspaper.

But arriving soon, to add support, in theory at least, is the coalition government's Localism Bill. There is nothing more local that the local newspaper. No local newspaper could mean no local community. That's why charity law is presently very relevant to newspaper ownership.

What opportunities?

Will there be opportunities for those seeking a charitable or a different status for regional and local news organisations? The good news for this is that there are examples in different but linked industries – and serving local democracy through the adequate scrutiny of local authorities and the need for reporting of local matters of interest is surely an issue with which few would disagree. The current UK coalition government has made great store by its desire for its 'Big Society' whereby the nation's citizens help make things happen that might not otherwise be achieved. Ensuring the survival of a level of local and regional scrutiny is arguably as major a 'Big Society' subject as there could be.

UK consumer magazine *Which?* sells some 500,000 copies a month, has 200,000 online subscribers – and is owned by the eponymous charity, formerly known as Consumers' Association. It is a highly successful business whose profits are covenanted to its charitable side that campaigns on behalf of all consumers. It is perhaps the best of all models for regional and local newspapers. The magazine is opinionated yet independent, with its opinions being based on sound evidence and independent research. But importantly it operates with a huge degree of retention of sales. Readers, who become very loyal, have bought in to the message of fighting for the consumer that Which? has developed over its near fifty-four-year history. They see their subscriptions going to a worthwhile cause.

Theatrical trusts, which manage many provincial theatres around the UK, enjoy the benefits of charitable status yet seek to entertain, inform, and stimulate their audiences, often in a provocative manner.

Newspapers that sought to have public interest aims at their core of reporting the community, scrutinising it and investing in its well-being would be well placed to carry out similar ambitions. If they were underpinned with public interest principles and an adherence to transparency and ethical ways of working, this could form the basis of a new business model.

Lawrence Baylis transferred the *Maidenhead Advertiser* to the newly formed Baylis Trust because he did not wish the paper to be swallowed up by a larger group. He had talked of the 'standing menace' posed to small, family-owned provincial weekly papers by large newspaper groups and of the importance of keeping alive what he saw as the 'invaluable' tradition of public service established by papers like the *Advertiser*. He believed that the formation of the trust would protect the paper and his analysis has proved correct.

He directed that the Baylis Trust would own the *Advertiser* in its entirety and that its profits should be used for charitable donations, mainly in its local area. He wanted it to continue as an essential element of the community it served. It seems to have worked. Since 1962 funds of £12.5m have been established, allowing for the distribution of often more than £500,000 annually to around 100 local good causes, many receiving repeat grants annually.

Even in the tough year of 2009/10 more than £200,000 of grants were made, despite the newspaper losing £284,000 on a turnover of £4.5m in 2008/09. Since then its performance has improved, with an operating profit of £42,000 over the following twelve months. The trustees at the time were cautious, with signs of optimism about the future: 'Whilst there are some small signs of encouragement, the organisation will continue to look to reduce its costs where possible and invest in areas of the business where it is felt progress can be made, even in these difficult times.'

What has clearly been of help to the trust is that local readers know that their newspaper sales payments, the costs of their small ads, and their clicks on the *Advertiser's* website all find their way back into the local community – a strong selling message.

The newspaper's chief executive officer, Jeremy Spooner, said that ownership of this kind made the organisation better placed to take longer term business decisions. Its circulation figures in recent years have been in line with the general 5% decline trend in the industry but it still claims to reach 80% of all adults in its core area. When the newspaper was redesigned in 2009, its editor Martin Trepte said: 'In our research no one had a bad word to say about the *Advertiser*. Readers all liked it but some just did not buy it every week for reasons of time.'

This is a model that existing small altruistic family-owned businesses could follow, or one that bigger organisations looking to divest or downsize could adopt. But is it a model that start-up business could follow? Possibly if the new business is derived from an existing company or charity, but more difficult if the business is a pure launch from virgin territory, as these tend to be entrepreneur-driven with profits as a strong motive.

The opportunities offered by under-the radar business advertising described above would allow small new publishers to develop local public interest principles and guidelines for covering their chosen area objectively and accurately and then to apply for charitable status to develop local news production, both print and electronic.

The main obstacle to alternative ownership models in the UK is the status quo. The bigger groups are still generating cash for their shareholders, albeit in much reduced quantities, and still see value in their properties. Newsquest proprietor Gannet said in late 2010 that its UK titles were still very profitable and, although mergers are said to be being examined if ownership regulations change, as the coalition government has said they will do, there is no indication that the big four will do anything in the short or medium term to change structural matters dramatically. DMGT said in early 2011 that it remained open to offers for its Northcliffe chain, but no early sale seemed likely. It seems that only an intervention by debtors would provoke such an event and there has been no indication yet of that happening.

There remains a free-market attitude, too, which believes that news provision (notwithstanding the BBC) should remain outside of government assistance. Most existing businesses do not see the need to change while their newspapers maintain a level of viability, and they would clearly have serious competition issues if a newcomer with a more favourable tax and liability regime created by charitable status were to enter one of their market places. For even when a newspaper is trading in what may ostensibly be a monopoly market, and where rival publications have disappeared, the remaining business and competitive challenges are immense, whether they be from the BBC, hyperlocal magazines and websites, or straight lack of interest from potential readers. The prospect, therefore, of another entrant to their market and playing under different rules is the last thing they will accept.

There remains a free-market attitude, which believes that news provision should remain outside of government assistance

It may be that an owner of an existing small publisher could convert the business into a Baylis-style model, with public interest guidelines in its founding articles, but that would take a major philanthropic leap. The big four groups still see substantial worth in their publications and their values will be aggregated on their balance sheets. Smaller, family-owned companies will still retain hopes of passing down some assets to younger generations, so there is unlikely to be a stampede of opportunities. However, the Baylis example does show that local support can assist such a move.

A possible solution is for the return of the patrician owner or owners, from which all newspapers emerged in the eighteenth, nineteenth, and twentieth centuries, and to aim for charitable status if they believe the tax and perception benefits are worthwhile. But they would have to either buy an existing business or launch in a very mature market.

Unfortunately, the image of local and regional news businesses, often propagated by the businesses themselves, has taken such a battering over the last five years, and their financial health has been viewed as so poor, that there have been no examples of local consortia getting together to bid for individual businesses of the big four. Broadly, the groups still profess their franchises to have value when outsiders do not believe them. The gulf is wide.

In the UK the position therefore remains unclear. There are examples of different methods of structure and working, generally from abroad, that may be adopted, but none have taken the opportunity. Baylis offers the best route – but it will take shareholders of all kinds of sizes to make decisions that write down and give away substantial values if that is to happen.

References

Chisholm, J. (2009) *UK Newspapers: The Road Forward. A Discussion Document on the Future of the Regional Press* (London: iMedia Advisory Services).

Currah, A. (2009) *Navigating the Crisis in Local and Regional News: A Critical Review of Solutions* (Oxford: Reuters Institute).

Fowler, N, (2009) 'Local Government, the Courts and Regional Newspapers', private report for the Press Association.

— (2010b) 'Charitable Status for Local Newspapers', private report for the Joseph Rowntree Reform Trust.

— (2010a), 'Charitable and Trust Ownership of News Organisations, Regional and Local Newspapers in the UK', presentation for the Reuters Institute for the Study of Journalism.

Louis Baylis (Maidenhead Advertiser) Charitable Trust (2004/05–2009/10) Annual financial reports.

Newspaper Society (2004, 2006, 2007, 2008) Annual regional press surveys.

Newspaper Society (2010) Press publishers analysis.

Royal Commissions on the Press (1949, 1962, 1977).

UK Press Gazettes, various (1965–2010).

PART II

CASE STUDIES

4. Protecting the *Guardian* through the Scott Trust

Victor Keegan

Most newspapers these days are created by marketing opportunities. The *Guardian* was born from a political drama. On 16 August 1819 the 15th Hussars and the local Yeomanry charged a peaceful demonstration in St Peter's Fields, Manchester, which had been called to campaign for a wider electoral franchise. In those days the people of Manchester had no MPs to represent them while the small county of Cornwall had forty-four MPs. Eleven people were killed and hundreds wounded.

Among the witnesses to the battle was John Edward Taylor who worked in textiles but did unpaid journalism for the *Manchester Gazette*. When he discovered that John Tyas, the reporter for the London *Times* had been arrested he and his friend Archibald Prentice wrote a report which they sent to *The Times*. It was taken up in a *Times* leader which, in the words of the *Guardian's* historian David Ayerst, 'turned a Manchester demonstration into a national atrocity story', known thereafter as 'The Peterloo massacre'.

It also convinced Taylor that the reforming movement needed a newspaper of its own. He persuaded eleven men, all involved in the textile industry, to put up to £100 each to back him as editor and sole proprietor. Interest – at 5% – was to be paid only if the paper could afford it and in the event of failure there was to be no claim against Taylor – an early hint of the not-for-dividend spirit that was to imbue the Scott Trust many years later. The original paper was not set up primarily to make money – though it had, of course, to pay its way – but to achieve social change. Most of the founding principles with which the paper was launched in 1821 – including civil and religious liberty, the fair reporting of both sides in parliamentary debates, and just principles of political economy – are still recognisable today in the injunction given to every new editor to carry on in the spirit of 'heretofore'.

The *Manchester Guardian*, as it was then called, owed its existence to John Edward Taylor (the first) supported later by his son John Edward

Taylor (the second), a very wealthy man, whose death prompted an ownership crisis because of a potential conflict between Taylor's desire to have the paper sold on special terms to his long-serving editor C P Scott and the duty of trustees to get the maximum price for the residual legatees (four nephews of Scott's). It was John Edward Taylor (the second) whose will suggested that future editors should conduct the paper 'on the same lines and in the same spirit as heretofore', a statement that has become embedded in the DNA of the newspaper.

The words were Taylor's but the principles he wished to perpetuate were already being practised by Charles Prestwich Scott, a nephew of John Edward Taylor (the first), who had been editing the paper since 1872. During a tenure that spanned fifty-seven years C. P. Scott earned the *Guardian* an international reputation. He led the paper through its controversial opposition to Britain's involvement in the Boer War in South Africa in 1899, its support for Home Rule for Ireland in 1886, and for votes for women among numerous causes he espoused.

In 1907 he became owner as well as editor when he purchased the paper along with other members of the Scott family following the death of John Taylor (the second). CP remains a towering figure not just for the *Guardian* but for the whole craft of journalism. His long leading article in May 1921 on the centenary of the *Manchester Guardian* with its famous injunctions that 'comment is free, but facts are sacred' and that 'the voice of opponents no less than that of friends has a right to be heard' is as important today as it was then.

Formation of the Trust

When C. P. Scott died in 1932, the Manchester Guardian and Evening News Ltd was inherited by his two sons, John Russell Scott and Edward Scott. Edward died shortly afterwards in a tragic boating accident on 22 April 1932 while sailing on Lake Windermere with his eldest son, Richard, then aged 15, who managed to swim ashore to safety. Richard, who later became a journalist on the *Guardian* (and also chairman of the Scott Trust), was to play a key role in the survival of the *Guardian* as an independent paper.

John Russell Scott was a shy person who did not like writing but he was totally committed to the ideal of guaranteeing an independent future for the paper. That DNA again. Edward had been worrying for some time before his death what might become of the paper if anything happened to the brothers because death duties demanded by the Inland Revenue could have killed the whole enterprise. The paper's argument to the Revenue was that it should be treated differently because it never ever intended to pay dividends. This did not impress the authorities. As David Ayerst noted: 'To the Inland Revenue this was not an obligation. It was a whim.' John Russell Scott, as sole shareholder, knew he had to do something. In an extraordinary act of philanthropy he decided against distributing the shares to his sons and nephews in favour of setting up a trust. Neither brother was rich because both of them felt themselves pledged to run the *Guardian* as heretofore in the common interest.

The Scott Trust was duly established on 10 June 1936 when all of the ordinary shares were handed over to seven trustees connected to the paper, all men. John received no financial benefit (except his £2,000 a year salary) but he kept the right to appoint and dismiss trustees. Although the avoidance of death duties that could have killed the paper was the triggering factor, it was also a decision of towering selflessness as the properties he was endowing to the trust – including the highly profitable *Manchester Evening News* – could have been sold off to predators such as Lord Beaverbrook for a very large amount of money.

This act of philanthropy has proved a dilemma for other newspapers or media groups interested in adopting the *Guardian's* trust model for themselves. First, you have to find someone prepared to give up their own fortune for the continued existence of the paper. Such people do not grow on trees.

This act of philanthropy has proved a dilemma for other newspapers or media groups interested in adopting the Guardian's Trust model for themselves. First, you have to find someone prepared to give up their own fortune for the continued existence of the paper. Such people do not grow on trees

The establishment of the trust in 1936 postponed the danger of death duties but did not remove it. In fact the prospect of being forced to pay inheritance taxes has hung like a Sword of Damocles over the *Guardian* ever since. In 1948 the trust had to be hastily redrawn when legal advice was that, because the 1936 document allowed the accumulation of income (even though it wasn't distributed to shareholders), it was liable to be taxed should John Russell Scott die while it was still in force. In November 1948 the trust was reformed so that the (theoretical) beneficiaries of the original trust – the so called settlors – handed on ownership of their property to the new trustees. David Ayerst gives this vivid description of the process:

> On the ninth the five beneficiaries appointed by the trustees were handed their individual cheques. Four of the five beneficiaries were grandsons of C P Scott . . . they were informed by a solicitor that they were free to do what they liked with what was now their absolute property, the whole of the shares in the Manchester Guardian and Evening

News Ltd. They then settled the shares on a new Scott Trust of which they and three others became trustees.

In 1975 a fresh crisis arose as a result of the Labour government's finance bill which was to introduce a capital transfer tax which included periodic levies on trusts that did not distribute their income. Editorially, the *Guardian* supported the more equitable distribution of wealth but not if it meant the destruction of the paper advocating such a course. To cut a long story short, the *Guardian* failed to convince the Revenue that it deserved special treatment and it was only after the editor Alastair Hetherington and others had personally lobbied the Prime Minister, Harold Wilson, and his Chancellor, Dennis Healey, that the threat was lifted.

Even this did not remove, or even blunt, the overhanging sword because such arrangements with the Revenue had a limited time span – in this case it was twenty years after the death of the survivor of a number of CP's great-grandsons or not later than the year 2030. Being a discretionary rather than a charitable trust, provision had to be made for the ultimate disposal of the assets at the end of the period. In 2008, with the termination period looming closer on the horizon, the trustees decided to act in advance to avoid the prospect of tax liabilities running into tens of millions of pounds, rather than waiting until the last moment when the tax regime might be less benign. They took advice that the best option was to change the trust into a limited company and then wind up the trust.

The trustees were convinced that this would preserve, indeed enhance, the *Guardian's* future security while continuing to ensure that trustees could not themselves benefit personally. There were immediate gains in terms of transparency since the annual report is now a public document and the memorandum of articles of association – unlike the original 1948 trust deed – is available for inspection at Companies House and the company's website. The board must meet modern corporate standards including regular appraisal of directors and the effectiveness of the board. It is now a company and the board are directors not trustees. The loss of trust status was disquieting for some trustees but it was resolved in what some might see as a typical *Guardian* compromise: the new body was called Scott Trust Limited, even though it is a limited company, so it could still be called a trust. The spirit of 'heretofore' was preserved.

The Trust in action

For most of its history the trust has been a passive institution, watching over the activities of the board and the editors but rarely intervening with management and never with editorial. The exception was the crisis year of 1966 when Laurence Scott, chairman of the company and a dominant trustee, took exploratory steps to merge the *Guardian* with

The Times without most of the trustees being informed. The move was aborted by the intervention of Alastair Hetherington, the editor, and Richard Scott, the chairman of the trustees. This episode prompted trustees to be more alert but they were still given remarkably little management information before they met. When I was asked to join the trust by Richard Scott in 1982, he warned me that I might not find it very exciting because of the low profile it then kept. That continued to be true for a few years. But under Hugo Young's leadership as chair the trust's role changed from passive acceptance to more active monitoring. This was mainly an unavoidable response to the rapid expansion of the group's activities to embrace not only existing papers such as the *Manchester Evening News*, but also the *Observer* (acquired under Hugo's watch), a string of television production companies (since sold), and Trader Media Group which runs the Autotrader family of car magazines which was then valued at £1.1bn.

In 1991/2 Hugo Young presided over a fundamental review of the relationship between the board and the trust, which confirmed the enhanced role of the trust, gave it access to more management information, and moved it towards more long-term strategic thinking. The review also considered some of the theoretical conflicts within the trust. The first was a potential clash between those who argued, as did most of the early Scott family years ago, that the paper would never make money and should be run as a public service (though in Hugo Young's time it was profitable thanks to the boom in recruitment advertising) and management members who thought that would be a recipe for financial indiscipline. This was resolved when Hugo dreamed up the magic words 'profit-seeking' for this paragraph of the review which remains the most succinct summary of what the trust is all about: 'To secure the financial and editorial independence of the *Guardian* in perpetuity; as a quality national newspaper without party affiliation remaining faithful to its liberal tradition; as a profit-seeking enterprise managed in an efficient and cost effective manner.'

The second potential conflict was that the top executives of the group board who were also members of the trust not only had an advantage over outside members in knowing everything that was going on inside the company but they were also, as trustees, being asked to sit in judgement themselves on what they did as executives, a clear conflict of interests. Editors have not always had automatic entry to the trust. Alastair Hetherington had to wait a decade before gaining admission. The trust decided to continue the practice of not automatically inviting the chairman and editor to join the trust and also ruled that executives should always be in a minority of less than one-third of trustees. Conflicts of interest between the roles of trustees and executives does not seem to be an issue within the trust anymore though it continues to be for the union. This may be partly because when Paul – now Lord – Myners was chairman of Guardian Media Group and also a strong proponent in the City of good corporate governance he voluntarily stood down as a trustee, thinking it was inappropriate to have both roles. He continued to attend meetings without having a vote. This was an important move though somewhat academic as the trust rarely takes votes, preferring to reach a consensus.

The balance of power

The trust is all-powerful in that it owns all the share capital of Guardian Media Group which owns the *Guardian*, the *Observer*, Trader Media Group, and investments in radio and other interests, but it chooses to operate at arm's length from the activities of its companies. It is injuncted not to interfere with editorial policy and has hardly ever done so except when editors themselves seek guidance, as Peter Preston (editor 1975–95) did after he had felt obliged to hand leaked documents back to the government during the so-called Sarah Tisdall affair. A similar hands-off approach applies to relations between the trust and the management, though it does occasionally act as when some years ago it stopped the *Manchester Evening News's* practice of taking sex advertisements in the paper, a decision that cost the group £1m a year at a time of declining revenues.

In recent years trustees have become increasingly immersed in monitoring what the company is doing so they are not suddenly landed with a decision to rubber-stamp that has effectively already been taken, as has happened in the past. The editor sits on the board of the parent company, Guardian Media Group, and the chief executive is a trustee so each knows what is going on.

Trustees have become increasingly immersed in monitoring what the company is doing so they are not suddenly landed with a decision to rubber-stamp

Meetings of the trust are dominated by detailed reports by the chief executive officer and the editor. The biggest editorial initiative of recent years has been expansion of the *Guardian* onto the World Wide Web and more recently the editor's moves to involving readers more in the operations of the paper through a process of mutualisation. In both of these cases the trust would have been informed about what was going on rather than the proposals being submitted to a vote.

The most important job of the trust is to appoint the editor since, being virtually unsackable (unless they do something gross) they tend to last a long time. It also appoints the editor of the *Observer* and the chairman of the company. Both Alastair Hetherington and Peter Preston served for about twenty years and the present editor is well on the way to a similar tenure. The *Guardian* has had only three editors in fifty-five years, a record unmatched in the rest of what used to be known as Fleet Street. This is unquestionably down to trust ownership. The *Guardian* has been blessed by seeming to have chosen the right editor at the right time. Peter Preston reversed a falling circulation and ushered the paper into a professional era while Alan Rusbridger's flair and deep interest in new technologies gave the *Guardian* a head start in the digital age. Four out of the ten trustees are now women. There are three independent trustees as well as Jonathan Scott, a member of the family.

Formal support for the *Guardian* within the trust has grown in recent years partly because editorial representation has grown (there are now four trustees who work or have worked for the paper as journalists) and partly because of structural changes. There was a time when the *Manchester Evening News*, which for many years supported the *Guardian* financially, was thought of as being almost pari-passu with the *Guardian* and its editor sat on the trust. But it has now been sold and the *Observer*, whose purchase the trust approved in 1992 as a kindred spirit to the *Guardian*, is important but secondary to the future of the *Guardian* which is now regarded unambiguously as the main focus of the trust's long-term thinking and is reflected in the recent financial reconstruction.

A significant proportion of Guardian Media Group's assets – apart from its huge investment in Trader Media Group and Emap – have now been put into a special investment fund. One available course of action in future would be for the group to invest more of its capital in a Wellcome Trust-style vehicle, the interest from which could be used to offset the losses of the *Guardian, Observer,* and website. This would provide a stable cushion for the *Guardian* but would also impose unavoidable financial discipline as the company would have to make sure that its losses didn't threaten the endowed income.

If all of the group's money goes into 'safe' long-term investments then it will buttress security but remove the chances of the serendipity that generated the bonanza success of the Autotrader group unexpectedly out of nothing – unless at least some of the money is invested in potentially lucrative but risky start-ups.

The Scott Trust also operates the Scott Trust Foundation, a separate charity with the same directors as the Scott Trust Ltd which looks after the archive and runs a continuous programme of educational activities at Kings Place (where the *Guardian*'s head office is located) and also the Guardian Foundation, its overseas training arm, that supports the creation and support of editorially independent newspapers around the world.

Participation

It is fair to say that the security offered by trust ownership has helped to make the *Guardian* a happier place to work compared with most other newspapers, although the redundancies associated with the recession and technological change undoubtedly sapped morale considerably. Most of the *Guardian* and *Observer*'s employees are proud to work for a trust-owned paper even though they find the trust's low profile a bit baffling at times. This contentment does not always spill over into the annual negotiations over wages, которые are often tense. Journalists would also like more power in influencing the trust and the choice of editor and employee trustee.

The trust has for many years invited a member of staff to be on the trust, though not as a representative of the employees able to report back but as a trustee like the others bound by the confidentiality of meetings. I served between 1982 and 1993 and was one of the last employees to be selected by the trust alone. On the last occasion employees through the union (National Union of Journalists) held a ballot to nominate their own candidate to the trust who was accepted even though the trust had had a different candidate in mind (who declined to be preferred over the elected person).

The trust reserves absolutely the right to appoint the editor; that is its main *raison d'être*. But there is now a large measure of participation. When the present editor was elected candidates who had put themselves forward were interviewed by a trust panel (drawn from the trust and employees) while the union organised its own parallel vote. On that occasion, happily, the choice of the trust coincided with the popular vote though there is no guarantee that this will always happen in future. It could be an awkward situation if the person chosen by the trust was not the popular choice as the chosen editor would have to work alongside someone known to be the popular choice.

Mutualism

Participation with staff is important and long standing. Participation with readers is new and exciting in a different way. The editor has seized the opportunity of the new tools thrown up by the web revolution – blogs, Facebook, Twitter, and other social tools – not only to open up a dialogue with readers but also to involve them in the gathering of news and providing material to help with investigations, as when thousands of readers voluntarily trawled through MPs' expenses on the web, a task that could not have been done by a handful of reporters. Where other papers such as *The Times* have set up a paywall, the *Guardian* allows free access to its material on the web. The hope is that revenue streams may one day be found for news and also the outpourings from podcasts, blogs, and the Twitter and Facebook feeds that writers have been strongly urged to exploit. It is doubtful if this could have happened on the scale it does without a sympathetic trust being prepared to invest for the long term.

Benefits of Trust ownership

There are two main benefits of trust ownership. The *Guardian* is often described as a not-for-profit organisation. It is really a not-for-dividend company and the money that would otherwise have been paid out in dividends – many millions over the years – has been available for investment and offsetting losses. This is a huge advantage. The second benefit is that the absence of an interfering proprietor able to sack the editor at will or of the baying voices of City analysts concerned about the fall in share price during a recession means the *Guardian* can genuinely look at the long term. The prime example is the paper's decision to build up a presence on the web. This has been extremely successful in terms of numbers as the *Guardian* is now the second biggest paper in the world on the web (with nearly 40m unique users a month) but not yet profitable. The trust was able to take a long-term view in not expecting early profitability in the belief that, if this was where newspapers were going, the *Guardian* had to be there in order to fulfil its function – a digital version of the 'heretofore'. The *Guardian* may not be making money yet but its views and news are reaching far more people around the world than at any time in its history.

The Guardian is often described as a not-for-profit organisation. It is really a not-for-dividend company

Guardian Media Group has in recent history made good profits that more than cover the losses of the *Guardian, Observer,* and website. However in 2009 the group lost £97m and in 2010 £171m (a figure that included some substantial exceptional write-offs). The group's combined cash balance and investment fund – set up to provide a buffer for the *Guardian* – stood at £261m, a decline of less than 3% on the year. Within these totals Guardian News and Media (i.e. the *Guardian,* the *Observer,* and the website) lost around £46m – an operating loss of £38m before exceptionals – in 2010 on a turnover of £220m and a similar amount the previous year. The losses were due to a combination of the effects of the international recession, the switch to reading newspapers online, and sharp falls in lucrative job advertisements in the newspapers. As a result, the *Guardian* had to make substantial economies including hundreds of redundancies – voluntary in the editorial department but compulsory elsewhere. The fact that no private shareholders are gaining from the downsizing probably made it easier for employees to accept the inevitability of change.

Trust ownership as such has no solutions to the deep structural problems but it does enable the company to avoid making panic decisions and to think for the long term. The effects of this are best seen in the paper itself (replicated, of course, on the web). Despite their losses the *Guardian* and *Observer* have maintained a very high standard of journalism throughout the recession, devoting large resources to international reporting, in-depth investigations (into tax avoidance, goings on at the *News of the World*, and involvement with the WikiLeaks saga to name but three) and analysis. A large number of pages were devoted to a review of the main countries of Europe in March 2011 – without any obvious payback in revenue terms. Although it is over a year since I left the *Guardian* I still feel tingles of pride in what is being achieved. Of course, things would look very different if the *Guardian* had not been the beneficiary of its investment in the Autotrader group – which no one at the time of purchase had any idea would turn into a billion pound company – but that does not alter the critical importance of trust ownership.

Trust ownership as such has no solutions to the deep structural problems but it does enable the company to avoid making panic decisions and to think for the long term

No one knows exactly where journalism is going as more and more people choose to read their news on the web where – so far – it is much more difficult to charge for the privilege. To have the backing of the trust at a critical period like this is clearly a big advantage. The *Guardian*'s early entry into web journalism has been spectacularly successful in establishing it as global brand in a way that could not have been dreamed about when it was a newspaper printed only in Manchester and arriving in the capital a day later (I know because I used to deliver it on my newspaper round). If C. P. Scott knew that as a result of a trust-backed initiative the paper he nurtured would be read by nearly 40m unique users a month around the world he would surely be a very happy man. The principles of heretofore have not changed; they have just gone digital.

5. Sustaining Independent Journalism through the 'Reuters Trust' (Thomson Reuters Founders Share Company)

Leonard Berkowitz

It is important to begin by saying that since it was constituted in 1941, the so-called Reuters Trust has never been a trust and the trustees have never been trustees, in the ordinary legal sense. It does, however, have a unique structure designed to preserve Reuters's independence while simultaneously making it sustainable. That structure remains in place following its acquisition by Thomson (which became Thomson Reuters in 2007).

The agency was started in the mid-nineteenth century and became a limited company in 1865, providing international financial and other news to British and continental European customers. The Press Association obtained the majority stake in Reuters in 1925, ensuring the availability of its information to the British press.

In 1941 Reuters, which was generally regarded as the leading international news bureau, was owned by the Press Association. It was acutely short of funds and increasingly subject to external influence and interference, particularly from the British government. Responding to these concerns the Newspaper Publishers Association agreed with the Press Association to provide additional capital to Reuters. They also agreed to regard their respective holdings of shares in Reuters as, 'in the nature of a trust rather than an investment' and to use their best endeavours to ensure that five principles were upheld. These became known as the Reuters Trust Principles. Subject to one point noted below, they remain in force today with only a few small, immaterial changes.

The principles, which the trustees aim to ensure are upheld today, are:

- that Thomson Reuters shall at no time pass into the hands of any one interest, group or faction;

- that the integrity, independence, and freedom from bias of Thomson Reuters shall at all times be fully preserved;

- that Thomson Reuters shall supply unbiased and reliable news services to newspapers, news agencies, broadcasters and other media subscribers and to businesses, governments, institutions, individuals, and others with whom Thomson Reuters has or may have contracts;

- that Thomson Reuters shall pay due regard to the many interests which it serves in addition to those of the media; and

- that no effort shall be spared to expand, develop, and adapt the news and other services and products of Thomson Reuters so as to maintain its leading position in the international news and information business.

The key principles are clearly the first (dealing with control), the second (addressing freedom from bias), and the fifth (requiring the maintenance and development of the news and information business).

By 1983/4, the Reuters business had changed radically. While maintaining and developing its news agency, it had also created a rapidly growing and extremely profitable business providing financial information and foreign exchange dealing facilities. The shareholders (now represented, in addition, by the Australian Associated Press and New Zealand Press Association) were eager to capitalise on these developments. As a consequence it was decided that Reuters should be floated on the stock market. It was accepted that the preservation of the trust and trust principles in an appropriate form were preconditions to any flotation.

The preservation of the trust and trust principles in an appropriate form were preconditions to any flotation

In the flotation Reuters was valued at around £800m. Proprietors sold on average around one-quarter of their holdings, raising in total £152m, leaving the remaining three-quarters in their hands. Reuters itself raised £33m by the issue of new shares. This additional capital and the ability to issue listed shares to fund acquisitions played a significant role in Reuters's development. Subsequent offerings by the proprietors raised another billion pounds, giving them important resources necessary to modernise and expand their businesses.

The structure which was adopted when the firm was floated (and which remains with a few modifications arising from the Reuters merger with Thomson) had five key features.

First, a company, limited by guarantee, and named the Reuters Founders Share Company, was formed. The same individuals were both members and directors and continued to be referred to as trustees. At the time consideration was given to its establishment as a trust and/or charity, but for various reasons a company in this form was deemed the best choice.

Second, a number of features were included in the Reuters constitution. The three most important were:

(i) an obligation on the part of the Reuters directors to exercise their powers to maintain the principles;

(ii) a bar on any person or group of persons acting together acquiring more than 15% of Reuters voting capital; and

(iii) issue of a special share, called the Founders Share, to the Founders Share Company. The Founders Share entitled the Founders Share Company to veto any changes to the Reuters constitution which might affect the rights attaching to the Founders Share. It could also take over voting control of Reuters if the trustees considered any person or group of persons was seeking to acquire or had acquired more than 30% of the voting capital of Reuters.

The third key feature was covenants by Reuters to the Founders Share Company to observe the principles.

Fourth, the main object of the Founders Share Company was to exercise the powers vested in it to secure compliance with the principles, so far as it was able to do so by the exercise of those powers.

Finally, the initial trustees were replaced over time by totally independent trustees nominated by a nomination committee. The nomination committee now comprises five trustees, representatives of the four Press Associations, two representatives of Thomson Reuters, and two judges from the European Court of Human Rights. There must be not less than fourteen trustees, none of whom may be employed by Reuters. Four of the current trustees are from the UK and the rest from Asia, North and South America, one from Australia, and the rest from different European countries.

It is also worth noting that the fifth principle, which originally referred to maintaining Reuters's 'position as the world's leading news agency' was amended in 1984 to refer to one of the world's 'leading international news and information businesses'.

The arrangements put in place in 1984 were tested and effective during the following two decades. There were attacks on Reuters's independence which were thwarted by the trustees' refusal to relax the 15% limit. Those attacks, if allowed to succeed, would in all likelihood have led to the demise of the news agency.

Conditions in the financial markets ultimately led to the merger with Thomson in 2007. The existence of the trust did shelter Reuters when the force of external economic and financial forces had placed the company under severe financial pressure but it could not protect the company from the need to respond to that financial pressure.

Reuters's business was largely and closely linked to financial markets. As a consequence it was cyclical and profited or suffered along with those markets. Thomson's business, while not immune, was much less volatile. While the provision of news was critical to Reuters's financial operations, its returns from media customers were also under pressure. There were various reasons why the merger made sense from the point of view of the trustees. The increased financial security and reduced volatility offered by the merger was one reason. Another was the attraction of the addition of Thomson's news business and the prospect of providing news to support Thomson's other activities. All this would clearly assist in the maintenance and development of the news business as contemplated by the fifth principle.

The decision to merge with Thomson involved careful consideration of the principles. The five principles are not all reconcilable but have to be balanced. The trustees had long recognised the potential for conflict between the first and fifth principles. Put in simple hypothetical terms, for example, could the trustees allow the business to decline or fail in circumstances where it could be secured and expanded by new ownership constrained by appropriate safeguards?

The five principles are not all reconcilable but have to be balanced

Following a careful review of the Thomson business the trustees concluded that the need for accuracy and freedom from bias was as fundamental to Thomson's business of providing information and related services as it was to Reuters. The cultures of the two firms in this regard were very much the same. This was reinforced by Thomson volunteering to apply the principles to the whole of its business. Critically, they also agreed to adopt the existing structure subject only to such changes as were necessary to enable the transaction to be consummated.

The pre-existing structure was substantially replicated at the Thomson Reuters level, with an exception for the investment by Woodbridge, the Thomson holding company. In the acquisition, the Woodbridge Company (the Thomson family holding company) was permitted to retain 53% ownership of Thomson Reuters, beyond the 15% limit of the trust principles. This exception lasts only as long as Woodbridge remains under Thomson family control. An additional fundamental safeguard was also added. Woodbridge covenanted with the Founders Share Company to support the trust principles and to exercise its voting rights in Thomson Reuters to give effect to that undertaking.

Today, the trustees remain actively engaged in securing adherence to the principles. They meet as a body twice a year in the ordinary course to receive reports from senior management on the activities of the Thomson Reuters Group generally and, in particular, in relation to those which may raise issues for the trust. If important issues arise at other times, they meet as required. Once a year they receive a report on compliance from the Thomson Reuters Board. At these meetings there is also a detailed report from the editor-in-chief on any issues which may have arisen or are likely to arise which could bring the principles into play. New business ventures which could raise such issues are also discussed. A detailed audit report on timings, corrections, and significant complaints (including relevant activities of competitors) is also considered. The trustees take an interest in the group's arrangements for induction into, and securing continuing observance with, the principles. They review the journalist's handbook with this in mind. The handbook has been publicly available on the Reuters.com website since 1998 and can be found at http://handbook.reuters.com/index.php/Main_Page. Trustees visit group offices all over the world to get a view of what they are doing, assess staff familiarity with and discuss the principles, and, on occasion, provide some local assistance. Each visit is followed by a report to all the other trustees and, where appropriate, to group management. The Founder's Share Company is funded through a covenant from Thomson Reuters to provide whatever funds are needed for its operations.

The trustees have no power to, and do not, intervene in the operations of the group. However, the chairman of the trustees is regularly in touch with the senior management of the group, and the high degree of trust between the management and trustees is an important ingredient in the effectiveness of the structure.

Looking at the question from the perspective of the group, the protection of independence is of limited concern under the present circumstances and is safeguarded should they change. However, as long ago as 1984 the directors of Reuters said in their prospectus that they saw the trust as an important manifestation of the company's commitment to independence and freedom from bias which would be reflected in trust in its products. As will be seen today from the Thomson Reuters website, the group still believes this to be the case, saying 'These principles are fundamental to our entire business' (http://thomsonreuters.com/about/tr_trust_principles/?view=Standard).

The existence of the trust and activities of the trustees may also help in promoting and maintaining standards in the group by providing a mechanism to keep them as a visible and active part of the culture.

6. The Poynter Institute Preserves the *St Petersburg Times*

Karen B. Dunlap

The search for new business models raises interest in an old structure: the three-decades' old non-profit ownership of the *St Petersburg Times* by the Poynter Institute. The model was designed to ensure sustainability, but not out of concern for cash flow. Instead it was created to help a Florida newspaper survive chain ownership and serve its community into the future.

Nelson Poynter's most quoted maxim said ownership of a publication or broadcast property is 'a sacred trust and a great privilege'. But in the 1960s Poynter's thoughts moved from ownership to succession. He wondered how to keep his newspaper independent and locally owned long after he was gone. Poynter rejected the models for media ownership of his time, including publicly owned companies and chain ownership, and he had doubts about long-term family ownership.

His lawyers explored various options and after years of searching he made a choice: he gave away his newspaper. In doing so he created a charitable operation that preserved the paper and created a journalism institute that has been highly influential on journalism practices in the United States.

The *St Petersburg Times* was his father's newspaper when Poynter began working there. The younger Poynter bought the newspaper in 1947 and guided it to economic and editorial strength. A change in the law in 1969 allowed a church, hospital, or school to own a newspaper. Poynter gave the *Times* to a school that he created and called it the Modern Media Institute. Trustees renamed the school in his honour after his death.

Today, the circulation of the *St Petersburg Times* is the largest in Florida and the Sunday circulation is the largest south of Washington, DC. The Poynter Institute is the most important journalism training institute not associated with a university.

Events in 2009 confirm the wisdom of Poynter's great experiment. During an economic downturn and while some media companies collapsed, the *St Petersburg Times* observed its 125th anniversary and won two Pulitzer Prizes: one for traditional, long-form feature writing, the other for 'PolitiFact', an innovative online truth-gauge of political statements. Paul Tash, CEO and chairman of Times Publishing Company, has said the ownership promotes the newspaper's commitment to journalistic excellence.

In 2010 the Poynter Institute observed its thirty-fifth year. The Institute offers seminars and conferences for professional journalists and media leaders, journalism teachers and students, and also other citizens interested in news. It is a non-profit owner of a for-profit news organisation. Dividends from the Times Publishing Company provide support for the school, along with tuition, grants, and contributions.

The school and the newspaper operate separately but with important connections. The Poynter Institute owns Times Publishing Company and that includes the *St Petersburg Times*. Tash is head of Times Publishing and chair of the board of the Poynter Institute. Nelson Poynter believed in vesting leadership in one individual who then selects his or her successor.

Mr Poynter envisioned a special role for the school. In 1977 he said, 'Modern Media Institute is going to be something big and important – it has to live modestly for quite a number of years, but its job is to help train the people who are going to help maintain the stability, the progress, the integrity of self-government.' The arrangement places a school that inspires journalistic excellence in ownership of a news organisation that seeks to achieve journalistic excellence on a daily basis.

That search for quality doesn't exempt either from the challenges facing the journalism business today. The US newspaper business model suffers from significant circulation decline as audiences fragment and from loss of classified ads to the internet. A deep recession compounded problems. In 2010 the Pew State of the Media report described an 'ugly' financial picture. 'Advertising losses, averaging 26% in 2009 (on the heels of a cumulative 23% loss the previous two years) left newspapers downsizing everything – the physical dimensions of the paper, the space devoted to news and, most painfully, their roster of news professionals.'

The search for quality doesn't exempt either [the paper or Institute] from the challenges facing the journalism business today

In 2008 the *St Petersburg Times* announced staff reductions, a decline that eventual went from 1,500 staffers to fewer than 1,000. In 2009 Times Publishing Company sold *Congressional Quarterly*, the highly regarded Washington, DC news service founded in 1945 by Nelson and Henrietta

Poynter. At the time, Tash said the sale 'lets the company extinguish its debt and advance its long-term goals in Florida'.

During that period the Institute felt the pinch of resources. News companies reduced their training budgets and that cut the Institute's tuition income. Reductions in staff and expenses followed at Poynter, as did increases in development and grants efforts. For most of its history almost all of Poynter's income came from Times Publishing. Now the Institute generates about half its income from other sources. This, too, follows Nelson Poynter's prediction for the school that he created. He believed that after an early period of building its reputation, the Institute would increasingly find support from those who value its work.

Like other organisations, the publishing company and the school are adjusting to media transformation. The newspaper strives to maintain customers and find new ones while developing its online sites and other products and services. The school creates new courses to serve journalists and media leaders, including bloggers, and those in online media start-ups. It also serves journalism students and educators and citizens who need to understand the news landscape. Poynter's major customers were once US news organisations that sent staffers. Now customers include many individuals who pay their own tuition, international associations, and public communicators who want to learn journalistic skills.

Like other organisations the publishing company and the school are adjusting to media transformation

Business problems have not been the only threat. Over the years the non-profit ownership arrangement faced two other significant challenges. In November 1988 Times Publishing Company and the Institute reacted to news that the Robert Bass group of Texas investors had bought company stock owned by Nelson Poynter's sister. Poynter sold the stock to her in 1947 at his mother's request. Her daughters inherited it and sold to Bass. During the battle that followed the Poynter Institute Board voted unanimously to reject the Bass group's offer to buy the *St Petersburg Times*. According to a history compiled by David Shedden, Institute head librarian and a Nelson Poynter Scholar, the Board's action was accompanied by a statement from Marion Poynter, Nelson's widow, who said 'Nelson spent the better part of a lifetime assembling defences against such assaults as these . . . there is no reason to give up the battle for independence, integrity, and commitment to the larger community'. After a two-year struggle the company was able to secure all its stock and announced an agreement with the Bass group on 17 August 1990.

A second challenge is the Institute maintaining its status as a non-profit school. Initially the Times/Poynter arrangement drew attention from the Internal Revenue Service as it tested this unique arrangement.

Examinations certified that Poynter met the standards of a non-profit school. Since then a few others have adopted this arrangement. The Nackey S. Loeb School in New Hampshire is most like the Poynter model. In 1999 Mrs Loeb founded the non-profit communications school that now bears her name. She was the granddaughter of publisher E. W. Scripps and the widow of William Loeb, president and publisher of the (Manchester) *Union Leader* and *New Hampshire Sunday News*. After her death in 2000 her two daughters donated her controlling stock to the school. Although Poynter is no longer unique in its ownership structure, the Institute still takes care in maintaining its approved status.

These challenges underscore the need for sound structures and prudent management. So often the Times/Poynter arrangement looks easy to outsiders. They see a business freed of public ownership and corporate pressures. They don't see that free of those pressures a for-profit still has to succeed in a difficult environment. They see a respected school drawing income from the newspaper it owns. They fail to see the press for additional funding similar to that undertaken by many non-profits.

In spite of difficulties, the Poynter/*St Petersburg Times* arrangement offers advantages. It allows the school to engage closely with a news operation in understanding newsroom and business issues and to conduct experiments with it. Years ago an experiment explored reader response to different news story forms. More recently the two worked together in teaching sessions on using new media tools for reporting on state government.

CEO Tash said the arrangement allows the news organisation to take the long view in its work and focus less on immediate profits. One example is the development of the free, youth-focused tabloid, *tbt** (Tampa Bay Times). Tash initially thought it would take three years or more to become profitable and said some other organisations would not have had the patience to make the newspaper a financial success. Without those pressures the *Times* built audience and profitability in two years. The long view is also apparent in the investment in regular investigative stories while many others are turning to lighter fare. Most of all, the arrangement encourages each entity to stay focused on mission.

There are a number of developments in the United States related to non-profit ownership of news media.

A slew of recent start-up news operations in the US rely on grants from foundations. ProPublica leads the group. Launched in 2008 it is largely funded by a three-year, $30m grant from the Sandler Foundation. Established news operations, including the CBS network's *60 Minutes*, carry its investigative stories, and in April 2010 the organisation won a Pulitzer Prize for a piece of theirs published in *The New York Times Magazine*. The Knight Foundation and others also fund new news channels but few see foundation support as a long-term financial solution. Most start-ups seek contributions but gain far less than the amount needed for a solid operation. Grants and contributions also raise questions about the influence of major funders. Much of the current funding comes from established foundations operating in the public interest. But what about philanthropists who fund news media to advance their special interests? It is easy to find biased media owners who press an agenda in small communities and major national news outlets. That's unfortunate. The problem shouldn't be exacerbated by news start-ups who plan a fair report but find that funding ties them to ideology.

Some look to a change in US tax laws to allow newspapers to become non-profits based on their educational value. Senator Benjamin Cardin of Maryland introduced legislation in 2009 but it has not moved forward. Questions include whether such a change would require newspapers to eliminate editorial pages and whether it would open a door for the government to interfere with news media independence.

Some look to a change in US tax laws to allow newspapers to become non-profits based on their educational value

There are reasons to think twice about the non-profit route, as mentioned earlier, even though the model has much to offer. Here are the some additional challenges:

You may have to give away your publication. Tash and his predecessors have been regularly approached by news executives lusting after Poynter's model until they are told they would have to transfer ownership of their newspapers to a school. Even owners who are willing to take that step face heirs (or stockholders) who might have other ideas.

The non-profit model still requires revenue and does not alter that necessity. This is the most important point in light of current financial challenges. It was discussed earlier but is worth repeating. The non-profit owner removes the burden of market pressure, but the for-profit news operation still requires significant revenue to report and deliver the news and provide dividends to the owner. The core problem of a business model for news remains.

It calls for trust. Nelson Poynter called ownership of news media 'a sacred trust'. Maintaining the system that he created calls for extraordinary levels of mutual trust. The leaders of each organisation must believe they are served by their own success and the success of the other entity. The school relies on the news organisation for dividends and the newspaper benefits from the ownership structure.

Legal ground must be tread carefully. In some cases precise wording in a will determined whether an ownership agreement was upheld. When Theodore Bodenwein prepared his will in 1938 to determine the fate of his *New London Day*, he could look to examples of what had not worked. Joseph Pulitzer's will said his *New York World* could not be sold, but in 1931 the paper was losing money and courts broke the will allowing a sale. Bodenwein took great care in the writing of his will making clear every plan and back-up plan. After he died challenges came from family and the government, but the will stood. Some attribute that to the specificity of the will. Changes in law and the acts of officials can undermine other efforts. The history of the *Toronto Star* presented elsewhere in this book gives some evidence of that. The Poynter model calls for clear regard to the law, including living up to the precise legal requirements involved in maintaining both a school and non-profit status.

Non-profit ownership is an important form for news media ownership, but it is not a panacea. Generally the model seems to inspire a keener sense of journalistic mission and a pride of history. It allows for less focus on quarterly returns and market ebb and flow. But owners still face tough challenges in generating revenue and finding new financial methods.

We will see more non-profit models in the near future. A few grants can start a business. The reduction of news staffs in the US means a lot of journalists are looking for a space to practise their craft, and many will choose the non-profit route. Owners will continue to turn to donors and foundations, as philanthropy remains strong.

Change will come in new forms of news services that we can't imagine now. Citizens will want to know what's happening around them and what's going on around the world. More and more citizens will assist in reporting and along the way they will focus on ownership and be willing to provide direct support. That will help some non-profits find paths to sustainability but many others will run out of funds and stop operating.

Government might provide some tentative relief, but concern about political pressure will prevent significant support. There will remain, then, a role for for-profit models, even though they are taking a beating now as audiences and technologies change. The rebirth of a profit model offers the possibility of a strong, steady income stream. To the degree that commercial models more readily draw broad audiences, this could help keep the masses turning to news media.

And that leads back to Nelson Poynter's model. Over three decades after its creation it remains worth emulating for those who approach with eyes wide open to the challenges noted here. Poynter's model combines the mission focus of a non-profit and the market-place focus of a for-profit. Future owners would do well in drawing on the best of business models and, like Mr Poynter, create new models that fit the times.

An earlier version of this report appeared in IPI Report: Brave News Worlds *(2011).*

7. Finding a Way to Protect the Principles of the *Toronto Star*

John Honderich

From what I know and have now heard about newspaper trusts, what strikes me is that each one of us has a different story to tell. Yet my sense is that there is also very much that is common in our collective experiences and it is with that perspective that I tell the story of the trust that owns the *Toronto Star* – Canada's largest and arguably most successful newspaper.

And while we all have unique stories to tell, I daresay the story of *The Star* stands alone. It is a fascinating story that begins in the 1940s with the will of Joseph Atkinson, the great founding publisher of *The Star*. Atkinson had built *The Star* to be Canada's largest circulation newspaper by pursuing a set of principles which have come to be known as the Atkinson Principles.

While the Principles were never formally codified, Atkinson had lobbied hard for half a century, preaching for a civil, tolerant and economically just Canada. In many respects *The Star* is to Canada what the *Guardian* is to Britain. Atkinson worried greatly about his beloved paper falling into the hands of those who did not share his vision. *The Star*, in short, was his life's work. Thus, in his will, Atkinson specifically said he wanted the paper to be run by people 'familiar with the doctrines and beliefs which I have promoted in the past'.

Consequently, he bequeathed all his *Star* shares to the Atkinson Charitable Foundation so 'that the publication of the paper would be conducted for the benefit of the public in the continued frank and full dissemination of news and opinions, with the profit motive, while still important, subsidiary to what I consider the chief functions of a metropolitan newspaper'. And you can imagine how that profit phrase has become a lightning rod for, shall I say, vigorous discussions over the past sixty years.

> '. . . with the profit motive, while still important, subsidiary to what I consider the chief functions of a metropolitan newspaper' (Joseph Atkinson)

That would have been the end of the story had not the provincial government of Ontario intervened. In an extraordinary move, the government passed the Charitable Gifts Act making it illegal for a charitable foundation to run an operating company. And to make matters worse, it made the legislation retroactive.

The fact that the government was conservative and *The Star* liberal was seen as the principle reason for the law. Indeed, at the time, *The Star* was the only major corporation owned by a charitable foundation. Thus the law became known as *The Star* bill.

Since the foundation could no longer own the shares, where would they go? Eventually the government appointed a Supreme Court Judge to hear applications from any group interested in buying the paper from the foundation. A price of $25m was set. It was then that the directors of the Foundation – who were also directors of *The Star* – formed what is known as the Torstar Voting Trust. Jointly they applied to the court in 1957 to buy *The Star*. Their principal argument – and the one that won the day – was that they were best suited to carry out the traditions and beliefs of Atkinson as enunciated in his will.

The Voting Trust made that promise to the court and, even in the offer of purchase, the families promised to 'observe and promote in its publications the doctrines and beliefs which the late Joseph Atkinson promoted during his lifetime'. They went even further. They said that they regarded 'the publication of *The Star*, a major metropolitan newspaper, as a public trust'.

Those arguments prevailed and the promises made still apply to the Voting Trust today. And, when the Torstar Corporation – the holding company that owns *The Star* today – was created in the mid-1960s, this legal obligation to uphold these promises was extended to apply to any director of Torstar.

So how are we set up corporately?

Torstar, since its inception, has been a two-tier share company with the Voting Trust owning 98% of the voting or 'A' shares. Only the voting shares can vote at the annual meeting and so, in effect, we decide who sits on the board of directors. Through a series of governance discussions it has also been codified that the CEO and Chair of the Board of Torstar must have the confidence of both the board of directors and the Voting Trust in order to continue.

Today the Voting Trust holds 31% of all Torstar shares – both voting and non-voting – on a fully diluted basis. That makes us the largest shareholder by a significant margin. And in the sixty years the Voting Trust has existed, not one single voting share has been sold outside the trust.

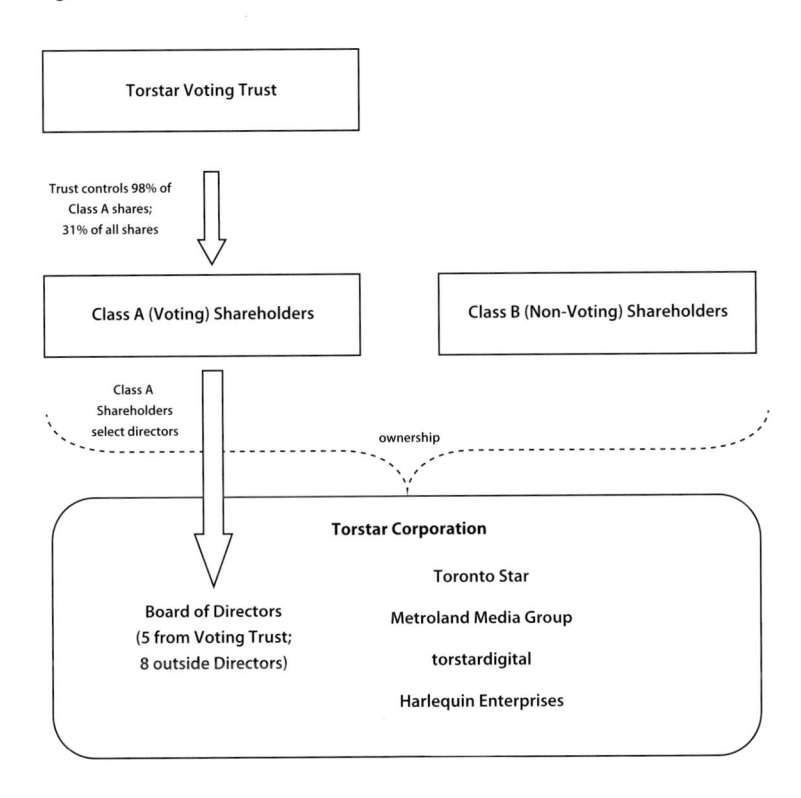

Figure 7.1 The Governance Structures Separate Control and Ownership

```
                  ┌─────────────────────────┐
                  │   Torstar Voting Trust  │
                  └─────────────────────────┘
Trust controls 98% of       │
  Class A shares;            ▼
  31% of all shares
┌───────────────────────────┐     ┌────────────────────────────────┐
│ Class A (Voting)          │     │ Class B (Non-Voting)           │
│ Shareholders              │     │ Shareholders                   │
└───────────────────────────┘     └────────────────────────────────┘
        │                                    │
    Class A                              ownership
  Shareholders
 select directors
        ▼
┌──────────────────────────────────────────────────────────────────┐
│                      Torstar Corporation                         │
│                                                                  │
│                         Toronto Star                             │
│   Board of Directors                                             │
│   (5 from Voting Trust;  Metroland Media Group                   │
│    8 outside Directors)                                          │
│                          torstardigital                          │
│                                                                  │
│                       Harlequin Enterprises                      │
└──────────────────────────────────────────────────────────────────┘
```

Parenthetically, if a voting trust member ever wanted to sell outside the Voting Trust, he or she would have to offer these shares first to other members of the trust. If there were no takers, then the member could sell the shares outside the trust – but the shares would automatically change into non-voting B shares. Only B shares are traded on the Toronto Stock Exchange.

Needless to say, for those in the public markets who oppose any type of two-tier share company, Torstar shares are not popular. There is, in the parlance, no takeover premium. Our response has always been: we are open and have fully disclosed what type of company we are. Investors should make their decision accordingly. The limitation on the sale of the 'A' shares has proven to be a very effective mechanism to maintain control. And I must say I cannot remember any occasion of capital borrowing or banking covenants where our corporate structure has been an issue.

Torstar today has a thirteen-member board of directors with a majority of directors – eight – not involved in the Voting Trust. But we have created a separate board committee, called the Toronto Star Advisory Committee, to ensure the paper is being run in accord with the Atkinson Principles. And half of the members on that Committee are Voting Trust directors.

So what does this all mean in terms of running *The Star*? My argument as chair of the Voting Trust is that those running *The Star* must meet two obligations. The first is to run a profitable newspaper for the sake of both the shareholders and the need to maintain editorial independence. The second is to ensure the promotion of Atkinson's beliefs and to ensure *The Star* remains a major metropolitan newspaper.

Do these two goals ever conflict? Absolutely. Remember, the Atkinson will specifically stated that the profit motive, while important, is subsidiary to what he considered the chief functions of a metropolitan newspaper. If one were to run *The Star* solely to maximise profitability and short-term shareholder value, it would be a different newspaper. We would not have as many reporters or as many news pages. Similarly, if one were to run *The Star* solely on maximising quality, we would have double the number of foreign correspondents and, arguably, considerably more reporters.

So I have always seen what I call a necessary creative tension between the twin objectives. It is hard to define and often hard to apply in real-life situations. But the fact that it is difficult has not deterred us from having some very lively discussions. And over the past sixty years we have had a pattern of editors and publishers, overseen by the Voting Trust, finding the appropriate balance.

I wouldn't want anyone to think the economic realities of the day have not come to play a significant role in our thinking. They have. And as newspapers have had to come to terms with a shrinking advertising base, we have had to make significant and often dramatic cuts in both staff and paging. But our goal has always been to protect the creative side of the business.

I wouldn't want anyone to think the economic realities of the day have not come to play a significant role in our thinking.

During my tenure as publisher we underwent three major strikes. In each case I was asked by the board if the action was consistent with the Atkinson Principles. And my argument always was: that in order to maintain the principles and stay competitive in one of the world's most competitive newspaper markets, we had to take this action.

There is no doubt this commitment has been derided by some, particularly those in the financial sector. Some have openly complained we are being run by the principles of a dead man. So be it.

Our primary audience is, and has always been, the readers of greater Toronto. And with their loyalty they have remained subscribers and maintained us as the largest and most successful newspaper in the land. And it has always been my sense that our commitment to the Atkinson

Principles has made us different and contributed to our success. We are a newspaper with a character. We stand for things. We crusade.

As Mr Atkinson said in a 1929 editorial: 'it is the readers of a newspaper that ensure its success – they and nobody else'. In short, the trust and our commitment to the Atkinson Principles have been a huge reason for our success. And that is why we have no plans to change.

8. Ensuring Independence at *Ouest-France*

Jeanne-Emmanuelle Gapsys-Hutin

Is it possible for a newspaper company to reconcile a not-for-profit structure with economic development? The answer to this question naturally depends on the legal situation in the country where the newspaper company is based but also, and especially, on the founding principles of the company. After all, opting for a not-for-profit structure is a choice. But why make such a choice? And, once this choice has been made, how can we make sure that it does not damage the dynamism or the financial credibility of the newspaper company?

The case of *Ouest-France* – the leading French daily with a circulation of 785,000 copies per day – is unique in France and it has confronted those questions and issues. In 1990 the newspaper decided to change its structure to become a non-profit association as a means to protect and foster the newspaper's independence.

Before detailing the steps involved in this complex evolution and its consequences for the newspaper, I would like to explain the newspaper's history because it shows why it was necessary to take steps to consolidate *Ouest-France*'s independence.

The roots of *Ouest-France* and its independence

At the end of the Second World War the French newspaper sector underwent major change. After the Liberation most newspapers were banned, quite simply because they had collaborated with the occupier, some going even as far as publishing Nazi propaganda. There was a deep and broad desire to rebuild an independent press serving the cause of democracy. So it was that press sector professionals who had refused to collaborate with the Nazis built new newspapers on the ruins of the old ones.

Ouest-France was established in 1944 and reflects this historical development. *Ouest-France* already had a highly distinctive character because it was the successor to the newspaper *Ouest-Eclair*, which had been established at the end of the nineteenth century by social republican Catholics. Its founders, Emmanuel Desgrées du Lou and Abbot Trochu, wanted to encourage Catholics to embrace the new Republic of France with its social democracy as Pope Leo XIII had instructed. *Ouest-Eclair* soon became the most popular regional French daily. For the founders, this success 'was not the result of abundant financial capital; it was thanks to the devotion of the founders and their acceptance not to seek personal financial gain from the paper'. Indeed, its founding shareholders included several priests and democratic abbots for whom the *Ouest-Eclair* was a way of expressing the ideal of reconciling a divided society by building a new republic respecting justice and liberty.

The Second World War created a difficult time for these aspirations. When Nazi troops entered Rennes on 18 June 1940, publication of *Ouest-Eclair* was stopped. Very soon, however, the occupying forces instructed that the paper be republished. The management board was divided. Some wanted to save the business by printing the paper and accepting the inevitable censorship, while others refused to entertain any type of collaboration. They essentially comprised two groups: one focused on equipment and resources; the other on an ideal.

In the end, *Ouest-Eclair* resumed printing with its title unchanged. But Paul Hutin, the general secretary and son-in-law of the newspaper's founder, resigned using the following words: 'to make the newspaper temporarily viable, we have sacrificed our ideals, and probably, in the end, the newspaper itself'. Paul Hutin had, on several occasions, denounced the dangers of Nazism and he knew that the occupying forces were going to use *Ouest-Eclair* to discourage resistance and spread Nazi propaganda amongst readers. Such a totalitarian objective was the total opposite of the social democracy embraced by the founding fathers of the *Ouest-Eclair*. And so it was that Paul Hutin joined the resistance, was arrested by the Gestapo and imprisoned, whilst the *Ouest-Eclair* became more and more a mouthpiece for enemy propaganda.

After the Liberation the *Ouest-Eclair* was banned and *Ouest-France* was established by Paul Hutin. He decided to continue the founding idea behind the *Ouest-Eclair* whilst learning from its problems – namely: confusion between business and principles, between means and ends. Hutin decided that it was necessary to create a partition between these considerations so that the future *Ouest-France*, originally established to serve democracy, would not become a channel for propaganda running against the initial founding ideas.

The first step consisted in recruiting people for the new newspaper who had refused to collaborate. Most of the shareholders were actually social activists involved in the Resistance and some had been deportees who survived death camps. They wanted to reconstruct democracy and to make sure that *Ouest-France* would act as an independent source of information.

As part of this Paul Hutin specifically excluded shareholder financial gain as an objective. In 1957, even though the newspaper was once again profitable, he obtained an agreement from all shareholders that they would not seek any dividends. The separation between founding principles and business was complete.

Paul Hutin specifically excluded shareholder financial gain as an objective

It meant that the shareholders no longer had any financial interest in attempting to influence the newspaper. In the words of Pierre Henri Teitgen, who was one of Ouest-France's founder members,

> *we were all asked to sign a pact of honour; to consider the new newspaper solely as the expression of . . . a tradition of human dignity, of human respect, of brotherhood, and liberty serving the best interests of our readers. We were asked to make an honour commitment to always consider the new newspaper as serving these ideals.*

Teitgen's commitment to ideals was deep. As a resistance fighter during the occupation he secretly prepared plans for the reform of the press to be ready for the Liberation on instructions from the provisional government in Algiers.

As the post-war economy improved, *Ouest-France* entered a period of prosperity. The willingness on the part of shareholders not to seek personal financial gain contributed significantly to its development – no dividends were paid out and all profits were kept inside the company. This meant that there were funds available to develop and modernise the newspaper.

Several investments were undertaken, including moving the paper to premises closer to the main road network and purchasing new presses. These investments were paid for using the newspaper's own funds. Employee work conditions were improved. The cost of the newspaper was kept down to boost circulation during good times and limit readership losses during bad times. Between 1957 and 1989, *Ouest-France's* circulation grew by 150%. At the same time, Ouest-France, as a publishing company, became an active participant in the media world by diversifying its activities.

But new developments were threatening its independence. When the first generation of shareholders retired, the financial pact of honour became more fragile. The founding agreement not to seek personal financial gain from the newspaper could be called into questioned by the new generation, not all of whom had experienced their fathers' combats. This risk was all the more real given that an unprecedented concentration had taken place in the French publishing world since the

1970s. Many newspapers, founded in the same spirit as *Ouest-France*, were purchased by financial or industrial groups. And *Ouest-France's* partners, who had not gained financially through dividends from the paper, would not be able to fight off the highly attractive financial offers that these groups could make to shareholders. This threat became all the more real when the law was changed to allow foreign companies to purchase French newspapers.

When the first generation of shareholders retired, the financial pact of honour became more fragile

Because the *Ouest-France* publishing company had significantly developed, its commercial activities took more and more importance. For strategic reasons the publishing company was obliged to acquire stakeholdings in a number of enterprises, for example, in the advertising sector with free papers of classified advertisements, book publishing, the new media and so on.

The newspaper company was in a delicate position. On the one hand, it was important that these commercial activities not make the newspaper lose sight of its initial principles, but at the same time, reducing the financial aspect of operations could well have endangered the newspaper. And so we had a dual situation where shareholders accepted relinquishing profit as good for the newspaper but understood that commercial activities, such as advertising, meant that these companies had to operate under standard business conditions.

This is why we considered that it was a good idea to separate the newspaper from other activities, and protect it from financial speculation. This was all the more important since developments in the legal and financial sectors caused us to conclude that the newspaper's original by-laws would not provide sufficient protection for much longer. We were convinced that the long-term independence was going to be compromised. The president of *Ouest-France*, François Régis Hutin, and his adviser Paul Museux, set to work to identify ways to secure the newspaper's future.

The two men carried out a number of searches in France and Europe to find an appropriate structure. The foundation used by the *Frankfurter Allgemeine Zeitung* seemed a potentially interesting model, but unfortunately it was difficult to apply under French laws since it required the involvement of the Minister for the Interior! And so, in the end, it was decided to set up a non-profit association.

A completely new structure

Thanks to a clever interpretation of French law, we were able to guarantee the newspaper's independence while setting out to make the group a credible and dynamic economic player. In short, the complete structure of the newspaper was changed. Specifically, the new structure devised to protect the newspaper's future consisted in the following. An association was created controlling 100% of the share capital of a civil society (SIPA). This civil society subscribed to 100% of the share capital of a limited liability company that purchased the *Ouest-France* newspaper from the previous publisher. Lastly, the publisher continued to operate the group's more commercial activities.

The process involved five important steps.

Step 1

Creation of the non-profit association to foster and protect the principles of humanist democracy. In order to keep the newspaper independent and safe from financial speculation it had to be placed inside a not-for-profit structure. In French law the 'Association' regime was tailor-made for this purpose. Specifically, the very first article of the 1901 law on 'Associations' clearly states that an 'Association' is an agreement whereby two or more people share, on a continual basis, their knowledge or activity for a purpose other than to share financial profits. 'It has a separate judicial capacity, is entitled to subscribe to the share capital of commercial company, and may run such a company.'

Setting up an organisation under the association concept to further the principles of human democracy was a way to guarantee that the original founding spirit of *Ouest-France* would be continued. The non-profit association's by-laws stipulate that its mission is to support and protect 'the spiritual and humanist principles defended by the founders in his spirits of service, personal disinterest and tolerance', to defend 'the freedom of the press' and to stimulate 'independent channels of information and communication'.

Setting up an organisation under the association concept to further the principles of human democracy was a way to guarantee that the original founding spirit of Ouest-France would be continued

This link between the two foundations (in 1944 and then 1990) is also expressed by the people involved: François Régis Hutin, the president of the group, is the son of the founder of *Ouest-France*, and he asked Pierre Henri Teitgen – the resistance fighter who was a founder member of *Ouest-France* – to become the first president of the non-profit association.

As required by the applicable legal texts company shareholders can, if they wish, join the non-profit association. In this way, they could continue to play a role in the newspaper's existence, and were guaranteed that *Ouest-France* would continue to defend the ideals and values to which it is attached.

The association now has sixty-two members. The association is open to members of the civil society who share its goals. These members are approved by a board of directors. Since first established, almost half of its members have had their mandates renewed. And thanks to the structure as an association, the initial aim of not being used a source of financial gain could be continued since, by definition, a non-profit association cannot distribute surplus cash. In fact, even in the event of the structure being wound up, any assets would be donated to recipients pursuing charitable activities.

Once the association was set up, *Ouest-France* was safe from financial speculation and its independence was definitively guaranteed since nobody can become a member of the association without the agreement of the board members. In this way, financial groups could not and cannot join the association unless the directors give their approval. Because the association does not have any shares, it can neither be purchased nor sold.

Step 2

An intermediate structure, the civil society SIPA (Société d'Investissements et de Participations) was set up to handle the future development of the newspaper. From a judicial point of view, the association was indeed entitled to directly own the limited liability company set up to run *Ouest-France*. But was this a good idea in economic and financial terms? For the newspaper, it was essential if it were to be able to borrow funds in order to invest. Sooner or later the newspaper would need to reinvest in itself or take holdings in other companies considered strategic for the development of *Ouest-France*.

Because associations cannot have any share capital it is very difficult for them to borrow significant funds. It was clear that, if the association were to directly manage the company running the newspaper, the arrangement would hinder the development of the newspaper because the company wouldn't be able to borrow sufficient funds for major investments. Therefore the partners decided to set up an intermediate company to act on their behalf in the financial sector. This led to the creation of the civil society.

SIPA consists of a general manager and directors, appointed by the association. The stake that the directors own does not actually belong to them; it is returned to the association on completion of their mandate. In this way, the group's financial managers make strategic decisions in a way that respects the association's guiding principles of humanist democracy.

Step 3

A limited liability company was set up to run *Ouest-France* and other firms with strategic and financial importance to its sustainability. SIPA would subscribe to 99.97% of this new company's share capital and would be the owner and operator. This new limited company was created with the intent to purchase the newspaper from the previous *Ouest-France* publisher. It left other assets and commercial activities in the hands of previous publisher. This process created a clear separation of activities. On the one hand journalistic activities are undertaken by the newspaper and, on the other hand, the more commercial activities are done by the previous publisher company.

Step 4

With the legal and operational arrangements put in place, the new limited company moved to purchase the newspaper as a going concern from *Ouest-France*'s previous publisher. This was a delicate operation. The first thing that had to be done was to set a price tag on the value of the newspaper. An expert appraisal was made to determine an uncontestable value and avoid any accusations of misuse of company assets.

Second, it was essential that the project be approved by shareholders representing at least 66% of the share capital in the original publishing company. On 9 April 1990, an overwhelming majority (90% with 5% abstention) voted in favour of this resolution during an extraordinary general meeting. A handful of shareholders initiated legal proceedings contesting the operation. At the end of a long legal case, their claims were dismissed, and the current structure that had been carefully prepared to comply with the legal texts was definitively consolidated.

The third task involved financing the transition. This was resolved by deciding to undertake a lease-purchase contract. The previous *Ouest-France* publisher leased its plant, property, and equipment to the new company, with ownership of the leased assets transferring to the tenant once they had been paid off. This occurred after seven years, in 1997, and at that time *Ouest-France* came to depend only on the association for the principles of humanist democracy.

As these major changes took place, personnel and their representatives were kept informed about the underlying reasons and goals and the Works Council approved the transformation. Because personnel employed by the previous company were being transferred to the new limited company, the work contracts had to be completely rewritten and we had to make sure that the acquired rights in pensions and other benefits were transferred.

This process of the transformation is illustrated in Figure 8.1.

Figure 8.1 Steps in the Creation of the New Structure

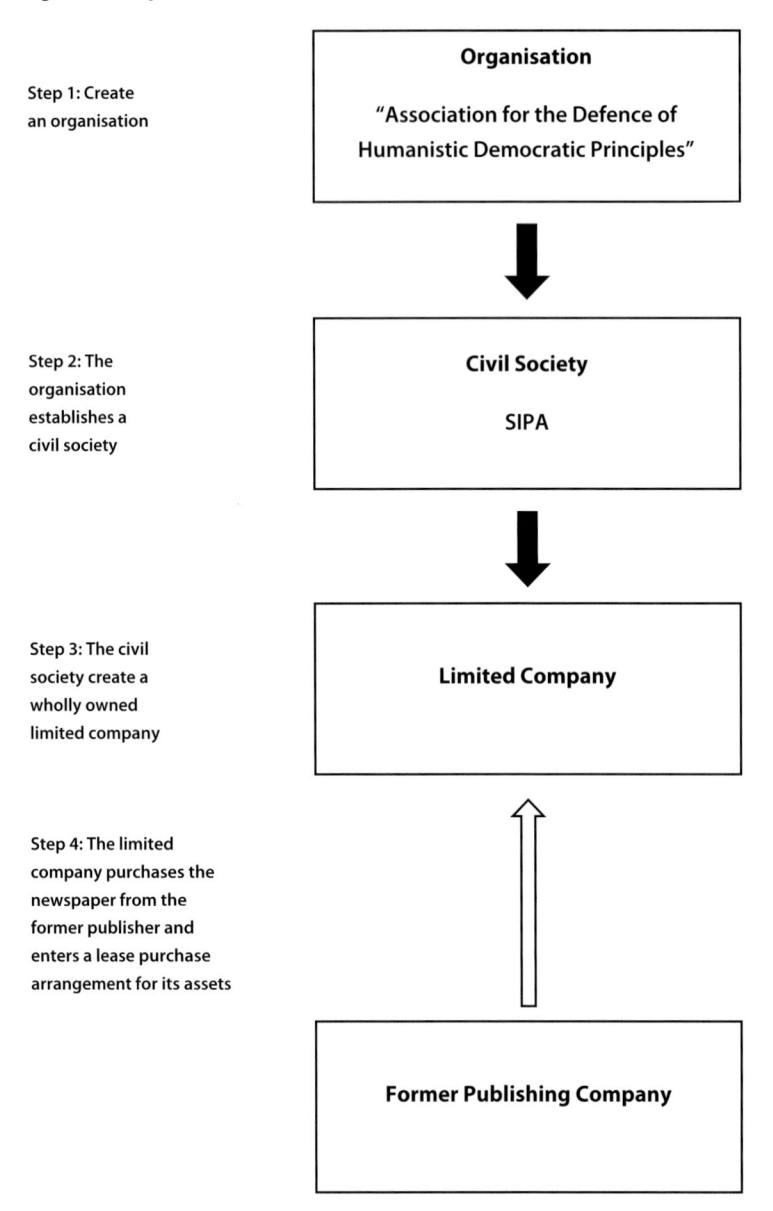

Step 1: Create an organisation

Organisation

"Association for the Defence of Humanistic Democratic Principles"

Step 2: The organisation establishes a civil society

Civil Society

SIPA

Step 3: The civil society create a wholly owned limited company

Limited Company

Step 4: The limited company purchases the newspaper from the former publisher and enters a lease purchase arrangement for its assets

Former Publishing Company

It is worth noting that this transformation did not impact the daily operation of the newspaper and its operational source has remained unchanged. The managing editor remains responsible for the overall orientation and operation through constant dialogue with the editor-in-chief.

The current structure and ownership of the group

Since the establishment of the new arrangements, the company has grown and developed, but it retains its basic protective structure. The organisational structure today is shown in Figure 8.2.

Figure 8.2 Current Organisational Configuration and Ownership Shares

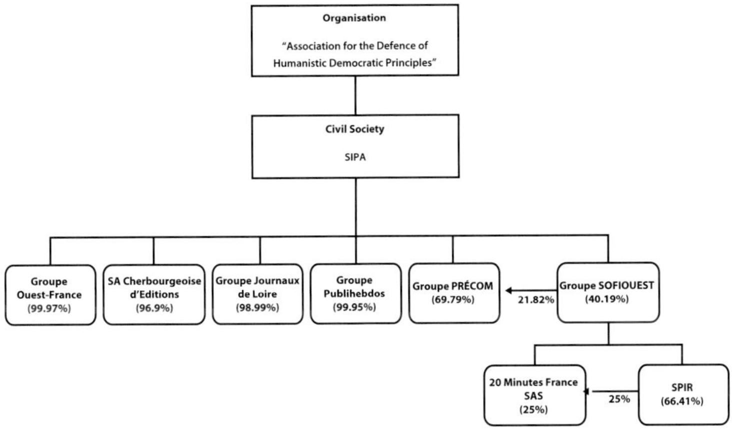

```
                    Organisation
              "Association for the Defence of
              Humanistic Democratic Principles"
                         |
                    Civil Society
                        SIPA
                         |
   ┌──────────┬──────────┬──────────┬──────────┬──────────┐
 Groupe    SA Cherbourgeoise  Groupe    Groupe    Groupe PRÉCOM   Groupe SOFIOUEST
 Ouest-France   d'Editions   Journaux  Publihebdos  (69.79%)   21.82%   (40.19%)
 (99.97%)      (96.9%)      de Loire   (99.95%)
                            (98.99%)
                                                    |                    |
                                            20 Minutes France        SPIR
                                                 SAS        25%     (66.41%)
                                                (25%)
```

SIPA thus owns publishing enterprises (the four groups on the left side of the figure), advertising activities (Précom), and other commercial activities (SOFIOUEST). It holds more than 95% of the ownership of the Ouest-France Group, Société Cherbourgeoise d'édition Group, Journaux de Loire Group, and Publihebdos (which owns sixty weekly journals and two printing companies). It owns two-thirds of the advertising operator Précom, which handles advertising for the newspaper and for Publihebdos. Précom is also the owner of a number of companies in the fields of public relations, poster advertising, local radios, and media consultancy. SIPA also owns 40% of SOFIOUEST (the initial *Ouest-France* company), which itself indirectly owns 65% of SPIR Communication, specialising in publishing and distributing (through Adrexo) free newspapers in France, as well as document printing (through IPS). SOFIOUEST and SPIR Communication jointly own 50% of the share capital of the free newspaper *20 Minutes*. Today, the SIPA press group counts a workforce of over 7,000, with 2009 revenue of €1.116m.

Conclusion

Thanks to these structures, and in keeping with the ideals of its founders, *Ouest-France* is a genuinely independent operation. A non-profit association set up in France under the law of 1901 can neither be bought nor sold, and it is therefore protected from financial speculation. As a result, there is no other risk than the well-known risks of the press sector.

The willingness of the association members to relinquish financial gain reflects the founding principles behind *Ouest-Eclair* in 1899 and *Ouest-France* in 1944. This was not an easy battle to win, but thanks to the desire and social commitments to serve democracy in the west of France by shareholders in 1944 and their descendants, it was to create this third foundation in 1990.

This orientation and the unusual configuration of structures enabled *Ouest-France* to overcome newspaper sector difficulties and become the most read daily in France and develop into a major media group.

This independence inevitably came at a financial cost for the newspaper, which essentially 'bought itself out' to set up a new association. In addition to the lease contract I already mentioned, there was also the social cost of transferring employees to the new company. But ultimately all these measures were taken to protect the rights of personnel. This editorial independence has very concrete and positive impacts on the newspaper; it also acts as a kind of umbrella in difficult times:

- Economic impact: It makes sure that profits remain within the company, that the newspaper is able to get through difficult times and can remain focused on the future.

- Social impact: It provides the editorial teams the necessary independence and peace of mind to pursue high standards in their profession.

- Ethical impact: It produces ever-growing trust among our readers, our most treasured possession. This can be seen in response to collections launched by *Ouest-France* Solidarité to help countries and people affected by natural catastrophes, including more than a million euros for victims of the Haiti earthquake.

We do not claim that our system could be used in all newspapers and magazines. We had the benefit of a special situation dating back to 1944 – made possible by shareholder willingness not to seek financial gain – which created a moral obligation for us to maintain that commitment. Combined with reader trust and the newspaper's reputation, the newspaper's prosperity made this project possible and successful.

References

Gaulle, C. de (2006) *Mémoire de guerre*, iii. *Le salut* 1944–1946 (Paris: Plon; 1st publ. 1959).

Hutin, F. R. (1970) 'Au service du lecteur', *Economie et humanisme* (Mar.–Apr.).

— (1990) 'Ouest-France franchit une grande étape', Ouest-France (10 Apr.).
— (2005) 'Le journal Ouest-France ou les voies de l'indépendance', Commentaire, 110.

9. Non-Profit Journalism Entrepreneurialism in the United States

Charles Lewis

There is a long tradition of financially successful, non-profit journalism in the United States, in some cases the incipient organisations substantially aided by timely technological innovations. And in recent years, in direct response to the severe contraction of for-profit, commercial newsrooms and its real-life ramifications, we have been witnessing the emergence of a new, non-profit journalism ecosystem of local and national reporting centres.

In 1846, the invention of the telegraph enabled four faraway US newspapers attempting to cover the Mexican war to 'actively collect news as it breaks, rather than gather already published news', and soon the Associated Press was born, incorporated in New York as a not-for-profit, tax-exempt, news co-operative. Today it has roughly 4,000 employees and delivers news around the clock to more than 130 countries and 1 billion readers, listeners, and viewers. AP reporting, including its photo journalism, has won forty-nine Pulitzer Prizes (Associated Press, 2011).

And of course, some of the best known publishers in the US are non-profits including (with their corporate names and their publications launch dates in parentheses), *National Geographic* (National Geographic Society, 1888), the *Christian Science Monitor* (The First Church of Christ, Scientist, 1908), *Consumer Reports* (Consumers Union, 1936), *Foreign Affairs* (Council on Foreign Relations, 1922), *Mother Jones* (Foundation for National Progress, 1976), *Harpers* (Harper's Magazine Foundation, 1980, although the magazine was a for-profit venture from 1850 until then), the *St Petersburg Times* (The Poynter Institute, 1978, although it was privately owned from 1884 to then), and many others.

In 1970 the Public Broadcasting System (PBS) began operation, and the following year National Public Radio (NPR) went on the air. Both began with government and philanthropic foundation and individual 'donors like you' funding, which is what sustains them now. Their high-quality programming, from *Frontline* and *The News Hour* to *All Things Considered* and *Morning Edition*, has won numerous journalism awards. Today, according to their latest data, more than half the US population, over 170m Americans, use public media – via 368 public television stations, 934 public radio stations, hundreds of online services, education services, and in-person events and activities (Sefton, 2010). And few, if any, national news organisations can match the audience growth of NPR, which has approximately *doubled* its number of weekly listeners to 33m Americans since 2001 (National Public Radio, 2009; Everhart, 2009).

Against this non-profit media tradition and backdrop, and even more specifically within the small community of serious-minded, independent reporters, a rising frustration with the inherent editorial reticence and practical limitations of the commercial news media began to occur in the 1980s and especially the 1990s. Understanding the past decades of disillusionment is essential to understanding the recent bursts of non-profit investigative reporting entrepreneurialism by undaunted, determined veteran reporters and editors.

A rising frustration with the inherent editorial reticence and practical limitations of the commercial news media began to occur in the 1980s and especially the 1990s

Throughout the twentieth century, despite the arrival of new means of communication such as radio, broadcast and cable television and then the internet, the most original reporting and the most extensive, substantive public service journalism in America was initiated, supported, and published by newspapers. The courageous publication by *The New York Times* and *Washington Post* of the secret history of the Vietnam War known as the Pentagon Papers in 1971, and their and other news organisations' strong coverage of the Watergate scandal culminating in the only resignation of a sitting US President, Richard Nixon, was and remains the apogee of independent journalism in America. Those unprecedented events – along with muscular reporting about the US conduct of the Vietnam War by David Halberstam, Neil Sheehan, Seymour Hersh, and others, as well as the national news media's awakening about gross, long-standing racial disparities and injustices in the South and its subsequent close coverage of the historic civil rights struggle between 1955 and 1968 – altogether represent US history's high-water mark in the struggle between raw political power and democratic values, including freedom of the press.

But inherent and deepening financial tensions within the newspaper business itself began to become apparent. For one thing, many major

US newspapers had gone public beginning in the late 1960s and to those within the journalism profession it seemed as though increasingly, over time, faceless, out-of-town shareholders were insisting on higher and higher quarterly earnings at the expense of quality news coverage. For a brief glimpse into how this pressure changed things, consider what happened inside Knight Newspapers, which owned fifteen newspapers at the time it went public in April 1969. When the company's co-founder and editorial chairman, John S. Knight, was invited to speak to a gathering of Wall Street investors he reportedly told them, 'Ladies and gentlemen, I do not intend to become your prisoner.' He said that 'as long as I have anything to do with it we are going to run the papers. We are going to spend money sometimes that [you] wouldn't understand why, for future gains and we [do] not intend to be regulated or directed by [you] in any respect.' Not surprisingly, his company colleagues never invited him to another analysts meeting.

For eighteen years Gene Roberts was executive editor of the flagship Knight newspaper, *The Philadelphia Inquirer*, and during that time the paper won seventeen Pulitzer Prizes. But as the corporate obsession with profits increased throughout the 1980s he became frustrated and finally, in 1990, he quit. It was almost a 'prescription for suicide', Roberts said (in an interview in New York in June 2007), 'to keep the profits up, which were very large, 20%, 30%, depending on what newspaper you were talking about.'

> *That's a profit margin far, far above what the typical American business had. So to keep the profit margins up and please Wall Street, newspapers began eating their seed corn. And they started cutting the space for news, and then the staff that gathered the news. And at the very moment in time when computers were becoming competition and you had 24-hour cable television coming along during the same period, and newspapers were being challenged as never before.*
>
> *But many of the managers of newspapers looked at it [as though] there was no competition anymore, not direct competition with other newspapers. There are few competitive markets left. So they, in effect, began to speak of newspapers as a franchise which basically could give the reader less and charge more. And, of course, readers reacted to that . . .*
>
> *At a very moment in time when newspapers should have been responding to a changing world, digitalisation, all of this, instead of giving the reader more, we ended up giving the reader significantly less. And newspapers are becoming less relevant. And this is a tragedy for democracy.* (Roberts, 2007)

Today the *Philadelphia Inquirer* has *half* the number of reporters covering the Philadelphia metropolitan area that it had in 1980. And in the same period of time the total number of newspaper reporters in the Philadelphia area dropped from 500 to 220 (Pew Research Center, 2006). Nationally, Leonard Downie Jr. and Michael Schudson found in a study commissioned by Columbia University in 2009 that the number of newspaper editorial employees has dropped by 33% – from more than 60,000 in 1992 to about 40,000 in 2009 (Downie and Schudson, 2009).

Obviously there now are vastly fewer people today to report, write and edit original news stories about our infinitely more complex, dynamic world; fewer journalists to hold those in power accountable. The oldest and largest membership and training organisation in the world for enterprise journalism, Investigative Reporters and Editors, saw its membership drop more than 30%, from 5,391 in 2003, to a ten-year low of 3,695 in 2009. And entries for the Pulitzer Prize in investigative reporting are down more than 40% (Walton, 2000). To put all of this in worrisome perspective, at the same time as the historic shrinking of newspaper, radio, and television newsrooms across America over three decades starting in 1980, the number of public relations specialists and managers doubled from approximately 45,000 to 90,000 people (McChesney and Nichols, 2010).

From 1977 to 1988, I worked at ABC News and then at CBS News program *60 Minutes* as a producer. My next to last year at CBS, I watched and winced as the most respected producers – friends and colleagues I was proud to know and work with inside the hallowed network news division made famous by the likes of Edward R. Murrow and Walter Cronkite – were unceremoniously fired. Because I was relatively young and therefore cheap salary-wise, I was spared. Within months of becoming the chief executive officer of CBS Inc., Laurence Tisch in 1987 had 'launched the biggest single staff and budget reduction in network TV history. When the dust had settled, hundreds had lost their long secure jobs, news bureaus had been shuttered, and CBS was but a shell of its former self.'[1] There unfortunately have been even bigger single staff reductions since 1987; indeed, network television newsrooms are roughly *half* the size today that they were in the late 1980s.[2]

My particular interest had been very simple. Hired fresh out of graduate school (the Johns Hopkins School of Advanced International Studies) as an off-air investigative reporter by ABC News in Washington in the wake of the Watergate scandal and then later as a producer for senior correspondent Mike Wallace at *60 Minutes*, all I had wanted to do was to find an unfettered place to investigate and expose abuses of power. And while I had investigated literally hundreds of possible and important national and even international stories for possible

---

[1] Douglas Gomery, 'Tisch, Laurence, U.S. Media Mogul', Chicago: Museum of Broadcast Communications; www.museum.tv/eotvsection.php?entrycode=tischlauren.
[2] *State of the News Media 2010* (Washington, DC: Pew Research Center's Project for Excellence in Journalism; accessible online at www.pej.org), executive summary, 3.

and actual broadcast by the two respective networks, I had gradually come to a painful realisation. As Cronkite had once observed about his own medium: 'the networks, including my own, do a first-rate job of disseminating the news, but all of them have third-rate news-gathering organisations. We are still basically dependent on the wire services. We have barely dipped our toe into investigative reporting.'[3]

Worse, I had seen firsthand certain nationally important stories not pursued, certain well-connected rich and powerful people and companies consciously not investigated. In a highly collaborative medium, I had found myself working with managers I no longer could completely trust journalistically or professionally, especially if any public criticism or controversy might arise - a fairly likely occupational hazard for an investigative reporter. My job was to produce compelling, important investigative journalism for a national audience then of 40m Americans, but after the broadcast, if there was the slightest 'heat' it was excruciatingly obvious to me who would be expendable. My sense of aloneness and vulnerability was palpable.

On 17 October 1988, days before my 35th birthday, after an unusually gruelling and contentious story production process, the morning after my investigative segment led the broadcast, in the midst of a four-year contract, with a family to support, a monthly mortgage payment due each month, and no savings at all, I abruptly quit *60 Minutes*. Producers there usually retire, voluntarily or involuntarily – but hardly anyone ever just up and quits the highest rated, longest running, prime-time television programme.

Beyond my own recent experience at CBS, for many reasons I had become frustrated that major investigative reporting did not seem to be particularly valued by national news editors, regardless of media form. Occasionally I had seen investigative reporter friends' and colleagues' stories unjustifiably resisted, reduced, or rebuffed by their respective news organisations. National news organisations often seemed only to reactively report the various systemic abuses of power, trust, and the law in Washington – from the Iran-Contra scandal to the Housing and Urban Development (HUD) corruption scandal to the Defense Department's procurement prosecutions of more than 100 people; from the savings and loan disaster, including the related 'Keating Five' Senate influence scandal, to the first resignation of a House Speaker (Jim Wright) since 1800, all of which occurred in the mid to late 1980s. In Washington there was very little proactive, original investigative journalism about these or other subjects, and, equally galling to me, smug denial instead of apologetic humility by the national press corps despite its underwhelming, lacklustre pursuit of these major abuses of power and systemic corruption.

---

[3] Howard Kurtz, 'Anchors in an Unmoored World', *Washington Post* (27 July 2009), C5. This comment was made by Cronkite in 1966 to *Time Magazine*, two years before *60 Minutes*, which would become known for occasional investigative segments, premiered.

I had seen investigative reporter friends' and colleagues' stories unjustifiably resisted, reduced or rebuffed by their respective news organisations

Weeks after quitting, against all odds and the overwhelming advice of many highly intelligent, respected people in addition to friends of mine inside CBS, and while eschewing lucrative job offers from other TV networks, I decided to begin a non-profit investigative reporting organisation. I knew almost nothing about the non-profit world, had no management, financial, or fundraising experience, had never started anything in my life, and I also understood the bleak reality that most new ventures fail. Illogically, I hoped that mine would somehow succeed.

I asked two very talented, trusted journalist friends living and working in different media and on opposite coasts who did not know each other, Alejandro Benes and Charles Piller, to serve on the Board of Directors of this new organisation, and they agreed. I was chairman of the board and the executive director. In part because the 'investigative reporting' names had already been taken by non-profit organisations – the Fund for Investigative Journalism in Washington (1969), which provided Seymour Hersh with some travel money to break the My Lai story, Investigative Reporters and Editors (1975), and the Center for Investigative Reporting in Berkeley, California (1977) – I proposed and we adopted the 'Center for Public Integrity' as the new group's name. While it sounded a bit pretentious and maybe even a little odd, all investigative reporting seemed to be about, on some level, affronts to 'public integrity' and the way things *ought* to be. The Center for Public Integrity was incorporated in Washington, DC on 30 March 1989, its mailing address a PO Box. Months later the Internal Revenue Service (IRS) approved its tax exempt status as a 501(c)(3) organisation and on 1 October 1989 I began working as the first and only full-time employee, from the upstairs guest bedroom of my suburban Virginia home.

Soon we had an Advisory Board of distinguished Americans, including Pulitzer Prize-winning historian Arthur Schlesinger Jr., political scientists James MacGregor Burns and James David Barber, political communications scholar and then University of Pennsylvania Annenberg School Dean Kathleen Hall Jamieson, Notre Dame president emeritus Father Theodore Hesburgh, veteran journalists Bill Kovach and Hodding Carter, Harvard sociologist William Julius Wilson and others.

The question was: is there a way to create a modest attempt at a journalistic utopia, an investigative milieu in which no one would tell me what or who *not* to investigate, the final published story or report unfettered by time and space limitations? I was not out to change the world; I did not have an 'agenda' except a desire to conduct major, thorough, responsible journalistic investigations about the origins and abuses of power in relation to the public policy decision-making processes in the United States and, eventually, around the world. Then and today, as stated on the organisation's website, the mission is 'to produce original investigative journalism about significant public issues to make institutional power more transparent and accountable'. The modus operandi: to investigate macro, systemic issues of great public relevance, using a 'quasi-journalistic, quasi political science' approach, in order to publish sweeping reports about government and public policy distortions of democracy which also name names.

Is there a way to create a modest attempt at a journalistic utopia, an investigative milieu in which no one would tell me what or who not to investigate, the final published story or report unfettered by time and space limitations?

This idea, this model for a more thorough, macro approach to tracking those in power in Washington, would later be resoundingly affirmed in the new organisation's very first report, 'America's Frontline Trade Officials', which was presented at a well-attended National Press Club news conference, and was covered by C-SPAN, CNN, ABC News program *20/20* and many others. It disclosed that 47% of White House trade officials over a fifteen-year period became paid, registered 'foreign agent' lobbyists for countries or overseas corporations after they left government. This 201-page report, which I substantially authored, enabled me to more fully disgorge and tell the *60 Minutes* 'Foreign Agent' story still in my craw at that time. The report prompted a Justice Department ruling, a General Accounting Office report, a Congressional hearing, it was cited by four presidential candidates in 1992 and it was partly responsible for an Executive Order in January 1993 by President Clinton, placing a lifetime ban on foreign lobbying by White House trade officials. Clearly, this approach of systematic investigation and announced findings to the national news media worked.

But, necessarily, before that occurred, by May 1990 the Center had secured enough money to open its first office in downtown Washington, DC, from a foundation, some companies, some labor unions, and a consulting contract with ABC News (although for that first office lease, my home was required as collateral). The issue of perceived financial 'purity' and exactly from whom the Center should seek and accept money has been an introspective feature of nearly every board meeting since 1989. Eventually, beginning in 1995, for example, we stopped raising funds from companies and labor unions because of their direct economic interests in influencing public policy; the non-partisan Center does not accept donations from governments, corporations, political parties, advocacy organisations, or anonymous donors.

The first full year of operation, 1990, the Center raised and spent approximately $200,000. From late 1989 to 2004, cumulative Center revenues and expenditures were roughly $30m, more than 90% of that from foundations such as MacArthur, Knight, Ford, Schumann, Carnegie, Open Society Institute, Annenberg, Newman, and many others. No year was more successful financially than 2004, in which our fourteenth book, *The Buying of the President 2004* (Perennial/HarperCollins) was on the *New York Times* (short or extended) bestseller list for approximately three months. Revenues were $6.49m, and expenditures were $4.54m. In 2003 and 2004, the full-time staff reached forty people, with fifteen to twenty or more paid interns each year, and more than 200 paid contract writers, readers, or editors in twenty-five countries on six continents.[4]

Transparency and accountability have always been important values, especially with a name like the Center for Public Integrity. All major donors are disclosed, as are annual reports, annual IRS 990 disclosure forms for at least the past three years and names and brief bios of every employee.

No reporting project is initiated or final-approved for publication without the personal approval of the executive director, who functions essentially as both the executive editor and publisher. The earliest Center reports were issued on paper and distributed at news conferences conducted at the National Press Club; from 1990 to 2004 I held thirty-five of them, roughly half of them nationally televised on C-SPAN; Center findings or perspectives were covered in approximately 10,000 news stories in the United States and throughout the world.

In July 1994 the Center entered a very topical, bitter Washington fray, positioned as an 'honest broker' in the midst of the political battle over the Clinton administration's health care legislation. *Well-Healed: Inside Lobbying for Health Care Reform*, more than 200 pages and the work of seventeen researchers, writers, and editors, chronicled the activities of 662 health care interests, analysing and presenting everything from privately funded trips and 'revolving door' examples to campaign contributions, personal investments, and other information. The news conference was covered by more than fifty reporters plus seven cameras, including ABC's *Nightline* and *World News Tonight*, NBC's *Today Show*, CNN's *Inside Politics* and *Newsmakers*, and *The New York Times*, etc.

The first solely online reports began to appear in 1999, although the Center website went up initially in 1996. The first commercially published book, *Beyond the Hill: A Directory of Congress from 1984 to 1993. Where Have All the Members Gone?* (University Press of America) was released in 1995, and it revealed the post-employment practices of 350 former members of Congress. Center book exposés were selected as the runner-up finalist in the Investigative Reporters and Editors' (IRE) annual book award competition for 1996, with the publication

---

[4] www.publicintegrity.org, 'About Us' and under 'IRS Compliance' see the IRS 990 forms for 2004. The 2000 Annual Report actually covers the first 10 years of the Center.

of *The Buying of the President*, in 1997 with *Toxic Deception*, in 1998 with *The Buying of the Congress*, and in 2000 with *The Buying of the President 2000*. In 1999, *Animal Underworld: Inside America's Black Market for Rare and Exotic Species*, by Alan Green and the Center for Public Integrity, actually won the IRE book award. No author, group of writers, or publisher has been so consistently honoured for books for five consecutive years by the thirty-six-year-old association of 4,500 reporters and editors. Since it began operation, Center reports have won more than forty national journalism awards.

The release of reports on the web and occasionally in the nation's bookstores represented an historic change in the amplification and dissemination of the Center's investigative findings. The Center no longer had to depend solely on the news coverage judgement and goodwill of the news media to inform the public about its findings; now the Center was reporting directly to the public, and if traditional or 'mainstream' journalists also deemed it newsworthy, all the better.

The Center's investigative reports are probably best known for exposing political influence and its impact on public policy decision-making in Washington, DC, and in the fifty state capitals. We started out systematically investigating the conflicts of interest of national political party chairmen (*Private Parties*) and unpaid policy advisers to the major presidential candidates (*Under the Influence*), which no one had ever done. But soon we began to turn our sights towards the presidential campaign. Dozens of researchers, writers, and editors amassed and studied thousands of pages and half a dozen types of federal and state records in 1996, 2000, and 2004, to produce *The Buying of the President* exposés, the first political books to systematically examine the powerful special interests closely aligned with each of the major presidential candidates and published and available to voters weeks before any votes were cast in the primaries and caucuses.

The first book, serialised in *The New York Times*, provided substantial editorial basis for the 1996 *Frontline* documentary, 'So You Want to Buy a President?' and the various major candidates' 'Top Ten Career Patrons' lists moved worldwide on the wires. In the book's Foreword kindly written for us by Kevin Phillips, he observed that,

> In the thirty-five-year cavalcade of presidential campaign books that began with Theodore White's landmark *The Making of the President, 1960*, no one has ever concentrated on the quiet but just as critical influence battle fought with checkbooks . . . Documentation like this has never before been compiled and published in advance of the election being described. Never. And the spotlight is scorching.[5]

---

[5] Kevin Phillips, 'Foreword', to Charles Lewis and Center for Public Integrity, *The Buying of the President* (New York: HarperCollins/Avon, 1996), 1.

At one point, in 1996, *The New Yorker* referred to the organisation as 'the center for campaign scoops'. That same year the Center also broke, among other things, the Clinton White House Lincoln Bedroom fundraising scandal.

'Fat Cat Hotel' won the Society of Professional Journalists 'public service in newsletters' award, a first for the Center.[6] It listed seventy-five donors to the Democratic Party who had slept over in the Clinton White House, part of a systematic plan to reward major contributors. Separately, from 1995 through 2004, the Center developed a fifty-states investigative focus on corruption in state legislatures, which culminated in *Our Private Legislatures: Public Service, Personal Gain*, a national investigation of conflicts of interest by state lawmakers, displayed on the website.[7] That 2000 report, disseminated in embargoed fashion to a consortium of fifty leading newspapers in fifty states, won the IRE online investigative reporting award. We posted, analysed, and reported on the annual financial disclosure filings of more than 7,000 state lawmakers, exposing literally *hundreds* of apparent conflicts of interest. To my knowledge this was the first national investigative journalism about conflicts of interest and corruption in all fifty state capitals simultaneously.

In October 2003 the Center for Public Integrity published *Windfalls of War*, which included the major US government contracts in Afghanistan and Iraq, definitively revealing Halliburton, and its subsidiary, Kellogg, Brown & Root, to be, by far, the largest beneficiary.[8] For six months twenty researchers, writers and editors worked on the project, filing seventy-three Freedom of Information Act requests and even suing the Army and the State Department (and ultimately winning the release of key, no-bid contract documents). That report, which was prepared by the Washington staff of the Center's International Consortium of Investigative Journalists (ICIJ), won the George Polk award.

The Consortium was the first, and is still the only, working global network, now approximately 100 people in fifty countries, of some of the world's pre-eminent investigative reporters collaborating with each other to produce original international enterprise journalism. Indeed, the ICIJ-generated, original, investigative, online content – about such subjects as international cigarette smuggling, water privatisation, private military companies, climate change lobbying, the black market in blue fin tuna fishing, etc. - transformed the Center for Public Integrity into 'the first global website devoted to international exposés', according to the *Encyclopedia of Journalism*.[9]

---

[6] Margaret Ebrahim, 'Fat Cat Hotel', *The Public i* (newsletter of The Center for Public Integrity), 2/5 (Aug. 1996); www.publicintegrity.org/assets/pdf/pi_1996_08.pdf.
[7] Center for Public Integrity, *Our Private Legislatures: Public Service, Personal Gain*, 21 May 2000; http://projects.publicintegrity.org/oi/report.aspx?aid=614.
[8] Kevin Baron, Maud Beelman, Neil Gordon, Laura Peterson, Aron Pilhofer, Daniel Politi, André Verlöy, and Brooke Williams contributed to this report, written by Ms Beelman: *Windfalls of War*, Center for Public Integrity, 30 Oct. 2003. http://projects.publicintegrity.org/wow/report.aspx?aid=65.
[9] Mark Feldstein, 'Investigative Reporters', in Christopher H. Sterling (ed.), *Encyclopedia of Journalism* (Thousand Oaks, CA: Sage Publications, 2009), ii. 801.

Focused so intently on political influence and corruption in the US, it is probably not surprising that we also became intrigued with trying to find a new way of monitoring and reporting on corruption, government accountability, and openness around the world. That curiosity culminated in an unprecedented, 750,000-word Center report – by far the largest ever – published online in 2004, entitled *Global Integrity*, prepared by 200 paid social scientists, journalists and peer review editors in twenty-five countries on six continents. This massive project spawned a new non-profit organisation called Global Integrity with a more academic, social science orientation and quantitative methodological component and with greater and more diverse funding and capacity needs than the Center for Public Integrity. Since 2004 it has published very detailed, analytical, annual Global Integrity Reports and analyses about corruption issues in over 100 countries.[10]

The mark of a true institution is one that has been able to survive one or more leadership transitions. In 2004, after fifteen years at the helm of the Center for Public Integrity, I came to that sober realisation after passing a milestone birthday. At some point the founder simply has to leave the building, for the long-term well-being of the enterprise. I gave the shocked board one year's notice, but nonetheless, the Center's ensuing two difficult transition years following my departure were brutal to watch, frankly; my immediate successor was fired after seventeen months and was followed by a temporary interim director. Then the Board of Directors chose Bill Buzenberg, a veteran journalist and innovative news executive at newspapers and public radio for more than thirty-five years, as the fourth executive director of the Center for Public Integrity. It was a brilliant decision. The former National Public Radio London bureau chief and first NPR managing editor and vice president of news launched several new programmes, including *Talk of the Nation* and American Public Media's documentary unit *American RadioWorks*. Since his arrival at the Center in early 2007 he has demonstrated substantial talent, grace, vision, and leadership.[11] A few months after celebrating its twentieth anniversary, the Center for Public Integrity ended 2010 with annual income of $8m, a full-time staff of 50 people, and very exciting new plans to embrace the digital age with new technologies, a new online platform and vastly expanded revenue potential.

When I stepped down as Center executive director and wrote my very last email to the staff on 30 December 2004, with the subject title 'Thank You and Farewell', I implored:

> *The Center must always maintain courageous, fearless 'edginess' and a willingness to expose abuses of power, from Presidents to multibillion dollar corporations. But edgy and*

---

[10] www.globalintegrity.org.
[11] www.publicintegrity.org, 'About Us' and under '2009 Annual Report', 16.

> *compelling must also always accompany fair and accurate reporting at the Center for Public Integrity, and nothing beneath this standard should ever be published. There is no such thing as too careful when it comes to information gathering...*

'The stakes,' I said, 'are very, very high, just as the opportunities to create high impact national and international journalism are extraordinary. Don't ever let the bastards get you down or intimidate you. But also, don't ever, in any way, enable them to diminish your credibility as a truthteller.'

It is impossible to predict the longevity of an organisation, news or otherwise, to understand the precise moment when it has become a venerable, lasting institution, particularly in this temporal, fleeting world of shortening public attention spans, as founders, leaders, board members, staff, and their respective sensibilities come and go – whether for-profit or non-profit.

But ironically, amidst the commercial newsroom carnage, the thinner newspapers, the increasingly vapid TV newscasts, certain editorial values such as a dedication to original, accurate, substantive, thorough, fearless reporting suddenly stands out more than ever. Those values are the Center for Public Integrity's values, indeed literally its entire raison d'être, and in terms of various quantitative measures – annual revenues, number of staff, audience interest, international web traffic and news coverage, peer recognition in the form of awards, etc. – all of its numbers are still climbing upwards.

Most interesting, in recent years dozens of other, new, similarly serious non-profit journalism organisations have been sprouting up throughout the United States. For some of the boldest members of the current Diaspora of immensely talented journalists with nowhere to work, starting a non-profit, online news site is vastly more appealing than the much bleaker prospect of leaving the profession itself. The editorial freedom, excitement and sublime satisfaction of a journalist creating and running his or her own news organisation are palpable – even if the editorial, administrative, and financial management responsibilities are formidable.

Late last year the Investigative Reporting Workshop I began in 2008 at the American University School of Communication in Washington published the first comprehensive analysis of the new journalism ecosystem of sixty 'new and not-so-new non-profit journalism sites/organisations, providing citizens with vital information at the local community, regional, national and even international level, sometimes investigative, sometimes more explanatory, but all of it serious, public service journalism'.[12]

---

[12] Charles Lewis, 'New Journalism Ecosystem Thrives', Investigative Reporting Workshop, 29 Oct. 2010; http://investigativereportingworkshop.org/ilab/story/ecosystem.

The new journalism ecosystem includes at least 60 non-profit journalism sites/organisations

We found that thirty-eight of the sixty organisations had been created since 2006. Three of newest, most financially robust ventures were founded by donors themselves – ProPublica (Herb and Marion Sandler) in New York, The Bay Citizen (Warren Hellman) in San Francisco, and the *Texas Tribune* (John Thornton) in Austin, Texas. But nearly all of the new non-profit news organisations were actually begun by 'newsroom editors and reporters who seldom wore suits or green eyeshades, folks long on guts but with little or no financial, entrepreneurial or management experience'. At least eight of the organisations are start-ups, with annual operating budgets of $100,000 or less, which means that several experienced journalists are working for little or no pay to get their ventures off the ground, sweat equity. Some of these enterprises may fail, particularly during this difficult economic time. Two-thirds, or 443 of the 658 full-time employees at these sixty organisations, have prior professional journalism experience and roughly half (twenty-eight) of the non-profit news publishers have won awards for their reporting. Many of these organisations partner with the commercial news media, and the cumulative total of the annual budgets of the sixty non-profit organisations is between $80m and $85m, essentially contributions from philanthropic organisations and individuals.[13]

There are also evident sensibilities reflecting a beleaguered profession wanting to uphold its highest traditions and values into the future, and also take financial advantage of existing physical and technological infrastructure. Of the sixty organisations, fourteen are part of universities or separately incorporated but at universities, bringing in an educational dimension of inculcating the journalistic traditions and techniques to a new generation of reporters and editors. Half of the sixty analysed organisations have an editorial/ethics policy, which suggests some degree of conscientiousness and introspection about standards and practices. And in terms of transparency, 78% of the organisations disclose their donors, but only 22% (thirteen of sixty) post their annual IRS 990 form revealing annual operating budget and salary information.[14]

Finally, most of these local, regional and national journalism non-profit organisations have also come to realise that there is strength in numbers. In 2009, the Investigative News Network (INN) was formed, now consisting of more than fifty member non-profit news publishers and expected to grow in number and extend internationally. No one has ever attempted to organise and syndicate the best, purely investigative reporting output and talent of member organisations, but, among other things, INN is doing just that and much more. Stay tuned![15]

[13] Ibid.
[14] Ibid.
[15] Charles Lewis, 'Great Expectations: An Investigative News Network is Born. Now What?', *Columbia*

All of this energy and activity is being watched closely by the lions of the profession. Barry Sussman, editor of the Nieman Watchdog Project at Harvard University, was the special Watergate editor at the *Washington Post* who oversaw the coverage of Bob Woodward and Carl Bernstein. According to him, 'Great reporting is still being done by the traditional media, but there is very little of it. It is the nonprofit model… that shows the most promise. More than anything else I can think of, it will serve – is already serving – to hold leaders accountable and keep important issues in public view.' Sussman also noted that 'non-profit news organisations are important in another respect. The Watergate era made people see journalism as honest, worthwhile work. They don't today. The non-profit model, as it grows and strengthens and stays independent, could bring that spirit back and draw bright, idealistic young people into the profession. And wouldn't that be nice.'[16]

The ultimate winner, of course, is the public, provided with independent, in-depth journalism where it otherwise doesn't exist, wouldn't exist and, in multimedia, is in infinitely more accessible forms.

References

Associated Press (2011) 'History': www.ap.org/pages/about/history/history_first.html (accessed Jan. 2011).

Downie Jr., Leonard, and Schudson, Michael (2009) 'The Reconstruction of American Journalism', *Columbia Journalism Review* (Nov./Dec.), 32–3.

Everhart, Karen (2009) 'News Cycle Attracts Record Listening', Current (30 Mar.); www.current.org/audience/aud0906npr.shtml (accessed Jan. 2011).

McChesney, Robert W., and Nichols, John (2010) *The Death and Life of American Journalism* (New York: Nation Books), 49.

Meyer, Philip (2004) *The Vanishing Newspaper: Saving Journalism in the Information Age* (Columbia, MO: University of Missouri Press), 174, quoting from Dan Neuharth, 'John Shively Knight 1894–1981: A Tribute to an American Editor', *Akron Beacon Journal* (offprint June 1981).

National Public Radio (2009) www.npr.org/about/press/2009/032409.AudienceRecord.html (accessed Jan. 2011).

Pew Research Center (2006) *2006 Annual Report on the State of the News Media* (Washington, DC: Pew Research Center's Project for Excellence in Journalism), executive summary, 2; accessible online at www.pej.org.

Sefton, Dru (2010) 'Drive Begins to Defend Federal Aid', *Current* (13 Dec.); www.current.org/federal/fed1023millions.shtml (accessed Jan. 2011).

Journalism Review (Sept./Oct. 2009), 17–18; http://irw.s3.amazonaws.com/cjr_sepoct_2009.pdf.
[16] Charles Lewis, 'New Journalism Ecosystem Thrives', Investigative Reporting Workshop, 29 Oct. 2010; http://investigativereportingworkshop.org/ilab/story/ecosystem.

Walton, Mary (2000) 'Investigative Shortfall', *American Journalism Review* (Sept.); www.ajr.org/Article.asp?id=4904.

PART III

IMPLICATIONS OF OWNERSHIP

10. Conversations

During the course of the seminar on charitable and trust ownership of news organisations a number of discussions were held on developments in news organisations, alternative means of operation, and challenges to trust and charitable ownership and operation of news enterprises. These present important insights into the issues and challenges posed by various forms of ownership and control structures of news operations. This section reports some of the discussion in those conversations because they add important concepts and perspectives to the topics and examples in the first two sections of this publication. Biographical information about the participants is found at the end of the publication. Conversations are divided topically in the following sections:

- Start-up Digital News Enterprises

- Not-for-Profit News Organisations

- Foundation-Supported Media

- Charity Operated News Providers

- Trusts and Voting Trusts

- Saving Failing Newspapers

- What Should Policy-Makers Consider?

Start-up digital news enterprises

Some observers assert that internet and other digital platforms provide the mechanism for new journalism providers to emerge and provide coverage that is missing or declining in legacy media. How realistic are these options and what challenges do they encounter?

Robert Picard: The primary funding for start-ups – especially online ones – came from journalists who were awarded pay-offs when larger news organisations made them redundant. Out-of-work journalists started news companies because they still want to work in the profession. In addition, a variety of foundations are funding start-ups in local communities and at the national and international levels.

David Levy: The US is much richer in terms of start-ups, an interesting difference to be aware of in looking at the international start-up landscape. What might you be able to do in British cities where the current owners will sell/close them? Could you create an environment with a change of legal status for an existing newspaper such that someone else would be willing to take it and run it on a different basis? It would involve smaller amounts of investment than creating a completely new entity and involve saving an existing organisation by changing its structure.

Chuck Lewis: I hear things from European journalists who want to get started, with a half-dozen foundations hovering and expressing interest; there are folks wanting to get money from the EU for funds for Europe-wide freelance journalism. Not everyone knows what the others are doing and there may be changes in terms of philanthropy that I haven't seen before.

David Levy: The biggest donation that I'm aware of in the UK is for the Bureau of Investigative Journalism at City University funded by £2m from the Potter Foundation. It is the first UK experiment funded on a reasonable scale.

Chuck Lewis: When starting something new you need to ask: why is this needed and what purpose are you serving? It is a peculiar act to start something up from scratch in terms of work and commitment so you need a certain person who needs to be willing to do that and has a fire in their belly.

Here are a few useful tips based on my experience: an MBA may be helpful experience but it is not essential. Don't ever try and start things by committee. You need an alpha personality to drive things through and be in charge. There are issues of structure – but if you don't get the front-end basics worked out, you run into trouble: these aren't just questions of skills, but of interest. If you don't have that, the public can tell and they'll lose interest.

Karen Dunlap: Besides mission, the sustainability of start-ups is also crucial to think about – it is relatively easy to start something up, less so to maintain it, and retirement funds are not going last very long.

It is relatively easy to start something up, less so to maintain it

John Honderich: You have to ask 'where's the business plan' – they can run through half their retirement plans and go nowhere.

Chuck Lewis: And at the very least those starting an organisation need a general idea of who might be collaborating with you financially on this. What are the earned revenue potentials? Who are people who would give money for it? I was going to start a for-profit at the Center for Public Integrity, to investigate stuff with federal data, but then I was afraid that if I had an opinion about the data then it would affect marketability, which was when I went down the non-profit route so I could keep the soapbox version. There's an evolutionary process, where you need to talk to a lot of people, and it takes months and it's not imaginable that it happens any other way. Anything you think will take a certain amount of time; plan to multiply that time by two or three.

Chuck Lewis: At some point you have to go beyond being a start-up. Starting-up is a big worry, but there are also some quite complex issues after that. A lot of what goes on here is governance, how you grow and adapt to current day, and the organisation as a work in progress.

Not-for-profit news organisations

Not-for-profit news organisations are seen by many as providing advantages over commercial firms in terms of independence from profit demands and creating organisations to supplement or replace floundering news enterprises. How useful are they and what issues do they face?

Chuck Lewis: There's the movement to entrepreneurship by the non-commercial sector. The largest non-profits are becoming successful, and institutions have to adapt over time. Non-profit journalism is changing – new journalists keep their journalist background but have to watch out for business opportunities; new media opportunities in moving to video from text, e-books, etc.; technology is changing but we can't have this convoluted state.

Robert Picard: Non-profits are proving to be an interesting way of starting with the journalism first, news organisation second. The critical factor is the values you have because people will or won't collaborate with you based on them.

Chuck Lewis: The structures of these organisations are fairly relevant but also maddening. Most of these non-profit structures are run by journalist types, which can be limiting; a mature organisation adds other people. Like a trust, you have to have people with similar values but different perspectives on the board.

For the first ten years of the Centre for Public Integrity we put people who were not journalists on the advisory board because we were so suspicious and nervous of them. An investment banker who loved everything we did put up a $20,000 prize for investigative journalism. We went to the board to see if we could put him on the board. The co-founder, then the board chair, said that we couldn't have him: 'he's a millionaire'; 'it'll change the atmosphere'; 'this could be the beginning of the end'.

It goes back to values and principles. The culture of these enterprises is their unique feature – partly why they became what they became. Start-ups are different, but the issues are still the same about structure, governance, legal background, and the adaptability of this structure to financial or legal siege. There are tricky moments but part of the story is successful governance during crises.

David Levy: Traditional boundaries are dissolving; commercial organisations are looking for board members with outside experience and not-for-profits need commercial experience too. Not-for-profit or charitable ownership is not about entirely cutting oneself off from the market. All these organisations need people who want to compete, but also may want some kind of protection for their values and principles.

Chuck Lewis: At the Center for Public Integrity, the board and senior staff are about to get involved to get in advertising, with a new daily online platform called iWatchnews.org. This is the first time to have a concentrated effort to generate revenue, bring in experts and projections, and it will be a real challenge. This will be the first national non-profit investigative reporting centre in the US that has attempted to generate revenue from advertising. It might surprise a lot of people and make news. It is important because the issue is how long will the foundations support us? There are dozens of non-profits and foundations are feeling beleaguered. This is survival mode and one has to build other sources of income, such as an endowment.

David Levy: The central value for survival is adaptability – moving from a model that is completely dependent on the initial donation to a sustainable one.

The central value for survival is adaptability

Rasmus Nielsen: These are cases of charitable, well-run news organisations. There'll be others that won't be good across all three variables. Some of the others that don't have such good stories to tell might also be useful.

Lenka Setkova: Most examples [in the seminar and this book] are also about very established organisations that have been around for some time. We need more examples of the new and emerging landscape of start-ups. Start-up and very local non-profit initiatives may be relevant for trusts and foundations that do not have large sums to invest or perhaps have an interest in specific geographic communities.

Chuck Lewis: For a non-profit on a smaller scale trying to exist over time, it must overcome the thing called the Founder's Syndrome. At some point, the founder should leave the building. In small organisations you're not talking about an institution, but people. Finding the person to ensure a leadership transition from the founder is a challenge that is painful as hell.

Foundation-supported media

Support from foundations and charitable contributions from donors are used by some emerging and established news organisations. How does one decide what foundations or donors one should work with and what are the implications of such funding?

David Levy: Foundations need to think as much about demand as supply. There is a danger of foundations saying 'this is the content we'd like to see out there' without a clear view of who is going to use it. This isn't sustainable and tells us more about what the foundation is trying to do but without the genuine demand for something. Markets can evolve and people's tastes change but in trying to create a new form of content you need to be hard-headed about what difference it will make, which will largely depend on who will use it, together with a timescale for how long a commitment you can make.

Lenka Setkova: To ensure this reaches as broad an audience as possible, we should look at the whole spectrum of ways in which foundations can support the news – hubs where innovation can grow, infrastructure, or research to push parameters of alternative funding models (such as industry levies and tax concessions).

Chuck Lewis: I know of three non-profits started by the funders directly. In these cases the founders are the money people, not journalists – which is unusual (usually it is the journalists who want to keep on being journalists). The Sandlers were very political before ProPublica. In their governance, the chief funder is the chair of the board. It's a fascinating example. I wouldn't want foundations on the board; it'd make me very nervous about intervention.

I wouldn't want foundations on the board; it'd make me very nervous about intervention

John Honderich: As the owner, though, if you're putting up the money you want to know what it's going into.

Lenka Setkova: The case needs to be made to British foundations to know that a large grant can make a difference to news. The case needs to be more clearly made to UK charitable foundations about the importance of investing in growing a more pluralist and independent news media, and that this need not require large sums of money. For example, in addition to investing in independent journalism/news organisations, foundations can play a key role in strengthening the 'scaffolding' for quality news media through supporting charities that promote good practice, accountability, and transparency.

David Levy: Trust and charitable funding is a way of insulating organisations from some pressures, i.e. those exercised by financial markets. But there is also another kind of pressure – the political agenda of proprietors or funders. So foundations bring values, but also, perhaps, the strong views of their founders which can act in a way like a traditional owner, which can expose you to the same pressures as Murdoch et al. How can you separate the beliefs of particular personalities from an enduring commitment to certain values and standards?

Chuck Lewis: The Sandlers are now scrambling to find non-Sandler money for ProPublica. You have to get a percentage of support from other sources – diversity of funders is a legal issue.

David Levy: Room of independence from founders is as important an issue.

Chuck Lewis: There is an affinity process where the entrepreneur has to find folks that are not too intrusive or obnoxious. They may have a lot of money but be people you might not want to go with.

Lenka Setkova: It might be worth outlining different motives for why foundations could be interested in strengthening news media: for example, providing people with access to information that helps them to engage with decision-making processes, enabling people to find out more about their local communities (especially in the context of the 'localisation' agenda), scrutinizing powerful institutions, etc.

Mandy Cormack: Potential funders, that is, foundations, cannot fund something in perpetuity. There just isn't enough money around. Foundations are looking for a recipient that is already able to get going.

Foundations cannot fund something in perpetuity

David Levy: How much money does one need to make a difference in this space – a baseline?

Chuck Lewis: Once people start to give you funding then you think you're succeeding. You don't tend to have a number in mind. Most of the start-ups in the last few years, their annual budget is $100–200k, or $300–500k, partnering with five to ten news organisations and making an impact on substantive issues. CPI in its twentieth year had approximately fifty-five foundations giving roughly $6m. But whether your sources of revenue are earned or donated, it's important to have diversification.

Robert Picard: You can't make a lot of difference with just one or two staff. Funders have to commit $100,000 or more; that's the range when they can start having an impact.

Lenka Setkova: Foundations can also do a lot by influencing public policy, where a modest grant could have a significant impact.

Chuck Lewis: ProPublica is unprecedented. Most donors will give you a one-year grant, and you're happy for what you get, but it means you have to go through the motions again. They're not sure about you and what they're doing themselves; that's just the landscape that you're chasing after these places. If most people aren't giving that kind of money, then many aren't going to. I wanted to make the same level as I did as a

producer at CBS News *60 Minutes* and if I couldn't, then it might not have lasted. You need to raise the money, but also the timing of that money – cash flow and when it arrives – to be able to keep things going.
Karen Dunlap: For the long run, local engagement in the revenue stream may be useful to overcome long-run funding concerns. If you are to serve citizens, should they contribute? If the democratic ideal is of citizens needing information, then in some ways they ought to be investing in that.
Chuck Lewis: It's not easy to start up because the grants are easily available; most foundations aren't out there looking for the journalists. It's a labyrinth to try and understand who has the financial interest and wherewithal to support journalism out there. The concerns that arise from the origin of the money, I think, are sometimes mitigated by the fact that serious professional journalists are involved – it's their name on it, their reputation. Often funding also seems to be directed at public broadcasting, rather than investigative work.

How long will people think that there is a civic crisis? Foundations want to solve problems of the day, and then move on – this may be what mitigates against 'puppet'-type control: their short-term attention spans, existing patterns of giving – so journalists have a challenge to glean what their priorities are, and to also be nimble and adaptive for when those priorities change.
Mandy Cormack: Charitable funding works as a sequel to that story, to get them going and perhaps take advantage of the tax breaks in the system. But it doesn't detract from the tension between economic viability and purpose.

Charity operated news providers

Some organisations are operated for charitable purposes to provide news and information not available elsewhere and some observers suggest these may be mechanisms to augment existing news provision and replace types of journalism being lost due to financial considerations.

Karen Dunlap: News charities can be a bridge, given all the changes around us in terms of paywalls and new financial models. Until a newer, settled model appears, society still needs to be informed and charitable support can fill this information gap.

Society still needs to be informed and charitable support can fill this information gap

Juan Senor: Charity-run papers are a cause for concern as you get too much 'soft community', kumbaya-type news; good journalism is good business. A paper needs to stand for something and have something to say in order to make it viable. Without these two aspects the paper will be discredited; the concept underlying the product can be washed out.

There's a complete disconnect between product and creativity. Most journalists have to share the vision and mission of their editors. When you give them a charitable-specific mission, such as promoting communitarianism, the results will not be as innovative or genuine as they might otherwise have been had they used their own initiative. Newspapers are usually championed by one or two specific writers or editors with their own personal mission statement and this is a good thing.

Robert Picard: In the US charities are not allowed to own newspapers as most of us know them. The tax authorities take the view that you cannot have a newspaper that isn't political by nature. Congress is considering a bill to change tax laws to permit ownership but it would not be allowed to take a position in a partisan campaign.

David Levy: There seems to be some agreement on a quid pro quo-type settlement for increased transparency in exchange for charitable funding. There's the relationship with users in the form of local news intervention that contributes to serving people in an identifiable community. We can see that some of the examples we have been considering have a strong local base and then there is Chuck Lewis, who is more national in scope.

Does the charity aspect undermine the service provided to users? You can end up just making content and pushing it out to see what happens. Or we can see that there exists a more platform-neutral method, where reporting happens without necessarily having the vehicle to publish it. There remain the questions of transparency and standards. Whose needs are to be met – the producer's or the consumer's? Is there too much emphasis put on meeting the needs of investors and not readers?

John Honderich: Charitable status gives a break from the economic model and is a means to an end. The successful papers had good relationships with customers to begin with. Charitable status gives a tax break but if it is available to all it just leads the market to focus and push towards operating at a lower cost.

Monique Villa: Nothing bars you as a charity from being run like a business – the same things are in play with foundations as with business: accountability, metrics, and transparency.

Trusts and voting trusts

Most news organisations that involve trusts and voting trusts have been established firms for which trusts have been created to protect the organisation, it values or its practices of journalism. These can sometimes lead to tensions and conflicts with other organisational and journalistic imperatives as time goes by.

John Honderich: The idea of the charitable trust was meant to maintain objectivity or neutrality in editorial judgement. This doesn't exist in reality as the very act of choosing a story reflects a set of values which takes it out of the realm of impartiality. The best that can be hoped for is a fair assessment of the facts at hand. What is the point of a paper if you can't have a point of view? People associate with a paper's viewpoint. In the UK especially, people identify with a certain paper's view and for this reason it has almost become a fashion accessory. The same is true in Toronto. Having a specific viewpoint that is explicitly put is part of a path to success rather than an economic structure.

Robert Picard: You can't say that a trust leads to quality or holds it back. Trusts were put in place to preserve quality that was already evident in most cases. Then the question that is put to them is 'how do you go forward and sustain it?'

Trusts were put in place to preserve quality that was already evident in most cases

John Honderich: Under the voting trust that owns the Torstar Corporation we have regular meetings and a charter that sets up the seven voting trustees and vote according to the percentage of our respective shareholder interests. We operate by a simple majority-voting rule if necessary, but most often by consensus. Sixty years on, issues of succession are important ones. With the exception of myself, only two out of five founding families are still personally involved. So there is a challenge in maintaining the interest of all the families.

Each family operates in a different manner. The families meet independently of the board and send their representative. An example is that the matriarch of a family passed on voting responsibilities to each of her children for five-year periods on a rotation basis. At the voting trust level, the representative changes every five years, which creates tension in the family and is not exactly an ideal situation for both the family and the board.

Rasmus Nielsen: How does one deal with the issue of what happens if trust ownership seems to become a commercial liability? There's a possibility of head-on collisions between the long-run endurance of values and the short-run running and sustaining of the business –

such as the Scott Trust putting more emphasis on print, which seems unattractive commercially as we move into a digital world.

John Honderich: This creative tension is endemic and natural to the trust arrangement, particularly where there has to be a redefinition of some of the basic principles along the way. Taking a strike, for example, involves a certain redefinition of those principles.

Karen Dunlap: I think that we are beginning to see more on the horizon the possibility of real conflict, where you have to ask yourselves, are you violating something? In the case of Poynter, selling *Congressional Quarterly* was something we didn't expect that we would do. On the horizon, in the mist of transformation, things might move beyond theoretical conflicts.

Leonard Berkowitz: In the Thomson transaction the principles had to be applied to a particular situation; there was a conflict between two principles which had to be resolved.

John Honderich: [There are n]o examples of smaller newspapers that have followed the *Toronto Star's* model.

Chuck Lewis: There's the family fight within the Washington Times: the other side of successful family trust arrangements is the dark side of what happens when it doesn't go well.

> *The other side of successful family trust arrangements is the dark side of what happens when it doesn't go well*

Juan Senor: Family-run newspapers are very common in both Spain and Latin America where it is seen as a very viable model. These families have other non-news interests which can put a political label on the paper easily – they act as a sort of safety mechanism for economic and political objectives for local interests which supports local causes championed by influential families, although their motives are not always altruistic or clear. Most of the credible newspapers are family-owned with a clear division, which is an interesting prospect for continuity. Issues arise, however, if families don't want to carry on accepted traditions.

Robert Picard: Succession problems exist everywhere. In most businesses, two-thirds of companies do not make it to the second year; only 15% make it to the third. Of 1,500 companies that are 200 years old, only two are newspapers; most are breweries or wineries, so it seems incredibly difficult to keep a family newspaper going even as a voting trust that controls an enterprise.

John Honderich: Torstar trades on the Toronto stock exchange but we receive denigration from some analysts that we're not in it for maximum profit. But we lay out what we are and so if you invest in us, you know what you're getting into. There's no misunderstanding what we're about. In terms of long-term shareholder value – this is the best shareholder strategy – the return is far greater, as is the investment.

Chuck Lewis: The universality of these trust arrangements is important. I think it's stunning – in a heroic way – that family descendants and others have essentially sustained a vision over multiple generations to do quality journalism and that this has happened in multiple countries in different continents. That seems something powerful to know about and you don't hear too much about them nowadays.

Saving faltering or failing newspapers

Some observers have suggested efforts be made to save failing newspapers by establishing new types of ownership and operational structures. Are such moves a viable way to save journalism in those localities?

Neil Fowler: There are good reasons why newspapers are shut down. Nowadays newspapers are highly efficient entities, so when they do need closing there tends to be genuine business reasons that go with the closure. In Trinity Mirror, when they closed eight free papers in the East Midlands they would have preferred to transfer those papers to another owner but were unable to do so because lengthy and complex regulatory conditions made that impracticable.

Robert Picard: In cases where there is a succession problem, not a business problem, there could be room for this.

David Levy: There is a tension in how some media organisations cut costs – more standardised content, fewer local journalists etc. – but also we see the growth of hyperlocal news. There is a question about how well suited some large organisations are to do very local news. The fact that it is in trouble may mean that there is no market or rather that the existing strategy wasn't tailored for local demand and there may be opportunities to reinvent news organisations with more localised content. You have to be careful if someone wants to get rid of it, since it may mean that it really can't be viable but equally that doesn't necessarily mean that it has to die since it might be revived in a different form.

The fact that it is in trouble may mean that there is no market or that the strategy wasn't tailored for local demand

Leonard Berkowitz: I get a local council free-sheet which does tell me about local news but I also get a commercial freebie which is purely advertising-driven and has virtually no news in it.

David Levy: If you're considering charitable/trust ownership to take over a paper that is failing, the question is: why is it failing, can anything be done or is it a dead loss? Then the question is what is it about this form of ownership that can make it more successful than it was before – are you going to have any values or purposes, or external funding that is going to make it more successful than a purely commercial enterprise? In the short run values and funding are needed to get started, but what about the long run? Is the discussion of local funding/charitable status just a tactic to change the economic model and cost base? There seems to be a dimension of local ownership and involvement too.

Neil Fowler: There are co-operative models of ownership: *News on Sunday, Scottish Daily News.*

Robert Picard: There are issues of what happens when you have shareholders who are supporters, like those for football clubs; if they're all supporters you can get some strange managerial choices. It is one way of developing new capital. But can you have public subscriptions as shareholders and leave them to run news organisations?

J-E Gapsys-Hutin: There are dangers of one pressure group taking it over.

Robert Picard: Looking at various forms of ownership, one US problem has been in employee-owned companies. There comes a time when the employees didn't want to be owners and employees anymore and would sell out.

Neil Fowler: John Lewis [the retail chain] has the checks and balances in place for such issues and has become highly successful. From the outside, it seems like the employees do have a genuine voice.

Robert Picard: If you are trying save a paper by changing it into a charity, you are going to have to give it away. It won't be owned and operated in the same way afterwards.

Karen Dunlap: If you want to go this route you do need to think about legacy and what others who have interests are going to say. Have you clearly outlined what your values are and thought through structure so it is not a tax scam? In the case of *St Petersburg*, ownership was given to a school. Once you have figured out the ownership then you have to answer questions of how to run it a news organisation.

What policy-makers need to consider

If you had one thing to suggest that policy-makers take into consideration as they view the changes in news organisations sustainability, what would it be?

Chuck Lewis: They need to recognise the social roles of news organisations.
David Levy: That news matters in some way; it should be the starting point for any kind of intervention or treatment.
John Honderich: They should consider some kind of recognised tax exemption because of the democracy argument.
Neil Fowler: They should have a realistic view of what the news market actually is.
J-E Gapsys-Hutin: New kinds of news organisations involving telecoms groups are appearing and they are our competitors.
Robert Picard: That news and information serves social beneficial and educational purposes and should fall within the boundaries of recognised charitable activities.

11. What We Now Know about Charitable and Trust Ownership of News Organisations

Robert G. Picard and David A. L. Levy

Based on this review of charitable and trust ownership of news organisations it is clear that they can provide a useful alternative to other traditional forms of ownership. The research and cases here indicate they can be structured in ways that makes explicit commitments to certain principles and values, that they can provide a longer term focus than might be possible in many commercially traded firms, and that given sufficient resources they can provide some cushion against temporary downturns in the market.

The book shows there are many different ways to structure charitable and trust ownership and that those choices are influenced by charities laws and the willingness of existing owners to give up control.

Many of the cases examined here are commercially successful firms that have moved to a different footing and well organised not-for-profit enterprises that make important contributions. Questions of how much charitable and trust arrangements can be used in a moment of downturn to try to save or preserve journalism or new enterprises remain unanswered, however.

A number of conclusions emerge from this review and are important when considering these types of ownership and control arrangements and the opportunities they present.

The quality of journalism organisations is unrelated to the type of charitable or trust ownership. The research and case studies show that quality journalism can be provided and maintained within a variety of charitable and trust arrangements. Commitment to provide and preserve quality journalism appears more important than the specific ownership and control mechanisms put into place, although some forms provide more potential for reducing commercial demands or avoiding pressures on journalistic value.

Owners of established commercial news enterprises have incentives not to turn them into charitable arrangements. Transforming successful commercially viable news organisations – whether local, regional, or national – into charitable and trust owned firms is possible only to the extent that owners are willing to make the interests of the organisation primary. Willingness to give up capital and profits to the firm, and to sublimate personal interests, are necessary to make such a change. The inclination of owners to give up ownership, profits, and control in an established news organisation is generally low and firms whose owners have done so have been led by extraordinary individuals, some of whom have made the decision as part of their bequests. The incentives to keep ownership private and enjoy financial benefits are likely to keep most owners of existing enterprises from considering these types of alternatives as long as their news enterprises remain commercially viable.

Owners of established commercial news enterprises may find trust arrangements more attractive. Although many owners of established organisations may be unwilling to fully give up their enterprises, trust arrangements present a variety of ways in which owners can seek to preserve the values and philosophies with which they have operated after they exit the firm. For it to remain sustainable they must also leave the firm in the hands of energetic leadership in the form of competent directors and managers, who have sufficient resources, and a pragmatic approach to the strategy and business of the enterprise.

Charitable ownership and control tends to be found in smaller organisations; trust ownership and control tends to be found in larger commercial organisations. Size appears to matter in the choice of organisational form. Smaller organisations, whose capital and governance needs are lower, seem to be well suited for various charitable arrangements and both not-for-profit and commercial operations. As scale and complexity increases, the incentives of commercial operation appear better suited to providing large-scale capital needed for operation and growth and engaged and effective management, and rewarding those who provide it.

Trusts tend to be used to preserve the character and principles of news organisations. Trust ownership does not appear to be a means of creating new commitment to social principles and journalistic value but as a means of preserving commitments that previously existed in its owners and practices. The cases presented in this publication indicate that it is possible to infuse them across the organisation and to maintain them well past the departure of those who established them by constantly reasserting and emphasising their importance to the enterprise and journalistic quality.

Charitable structures and trust ownership does not shield operations from long-term changes in audience behaviour or economic downturns. Regardless of noble intentions, these organisations are not shielded from market and economic developments and management and must wrestle with the challenges they pose. News organisations whose audiences shift to television and internet for news face cost challenges in serving smaller audiences, whether they are commercial or not-for-profit enterprises, and may face income challenges because of them. Significant economic downturns affect revenue and force financial prudence and cuts on charitable and trust owned enterprises, just as for other types of news organisations. Reduced profit demands that may be in place provide some benefits in poor economic times but the necessity for fiscal responsibility will also lead to balancing budgets that may call for reductions in services and employment.

Neither charitable nor trust based arrangements can be effective or survive in the long run unless they are managed effectively and attention is paid to their economic well-being; that may require a willingness to adapt as well as to preserve. These arrangements require high levels of management effectiveness and significant attention to their financial conditions to ensure sustainability. Although they may provide a shield from some short-term economic pressures, they do not remove the necessity for nurturing revenue streams and operating with fiscal responsibility. As much attention needs to be paid to meeting the organisational requirements as to meeting the journalistic requirements.

Foundation support of news organisations is unlikely to sustain news operations over the long run unless a new business model is found. Because the interests of foundations vary over time depending upon their governance and programmes, funding for news enterprises provided by general foundations and community foundations cannot be expected to be a long-term solution to challenges facing news organisations. Those operating new organisations need to ensure their sources of funding are continually diversified to reduce dependence on any one source, including foundations. The future of news organisations is dependent upon evolving away from the mass media business model whose limitations are now readily apparent and directors and managers of charitably owned and supported enterprises, especially not-for-profit operations, need to pay attention to the evolution in the commercial sector because it will help inform their own possibilities.

Legal arrangements surrounding charitable status can affect what opportunities can be pursued; greater clarity in this area would be

helpful. In the UK case, as Neil Fowler demonstrates (see Chapter 3), the benefits of charitable status, particularly for local newspapers, could be substantial. As well as the financial aspects other benefits might include preserving titles that might otherwise go under and assisting in building a sense of community around a local newspaper. However the treatment of not-for-profit news organisations under UK charity law remains untested. One way to resolve this would be to create a test case of a local charitably operated newspaper or other news organisation that set out to deliver a clear public benefit. Ideally that would then allow the charity law in this area to be clarified.

Changes in trust and charitable arrangements can sometimes be forced on firms by legal action by board members and others related to the enterprise financially. Because these arrangements are based in law and policy, they must meet requirements placed on them by tax and charity authorities and carry out appropriate governance and fiscal responsibilities. Should laws change the requirements for charity or trust ownership there must be compliance with the new conditions or the form of the organisation must change. Similarly, board members and trustees must remain convinced the enterprise is acting according to its charitable, trust, and fiduciary responsibilities or they may seek to change or influence its governance through legal challenges. Thus contemporary arrangements cannot be seen as permanent, even though they may last for a generation or more and demands for better performance and greater fiduciary responsibility may be forced upon them.

Laws that permit charitable and trust ownership can be changed and can sometimes be used as a weapon against journalism enterprises by political figures. The legal bases and continued operations of these forms of ownership and control are dependent upon laws and regulations that permit and guide their existence and activities. Should charities, trusts, or tax laws be altered in ways that remove benefits that make them possible, it is possible that charitable and trust arrangements might become unviable and enterprises might be forced to change ownership and governance provisions. Independent journalism that holds power to account does not always maintain the support of political leaders. Charitably and trust owned news organisations are thus vulnerable to attacks on their activities by governmental officials who are willing to alter or misuse laws and regulations governing such ownership as retaliation for the activities of the media.

All charitable and trust arrangements require attention to their governance. Ensuring dedicated and knowledgeable supervision of charitable and trust owned news organisations requires regular attention to developing and maintaining active governing boards and processes that promote effective strategy-making, implementation, and monitoring of their activities. Absent the high financial incentives typically provided for directors and managers of commercial firms, maintaining the commitment, enthusiasm, and involvement of those governing charitable and trust news enterprises is vital.

These many and varied challenges to trust and charitable ownership are designed to provide a 'reality check' to those who see these new forms of ownership as a panacea to the problems currently affecting news organisations. There is a limit to what alternative forms of ownership can offer and each and every form has a mix of negative as well as positive aspects. However, there are strong grounds for giving more consideration than has been the case to date to these alternative forms of ownership, as one part of a portfolio of responses to the current travails of many parts of the news industry. When structured and staffed correctly, alternative structures can help keep news organisations focused on the public interest aspects of accountability journalism both at national and local level, avoid the short-term pressures of the financial markets which led some publically quoted news organisations to take on excessive levels of debt in recent years, and combine preserving the intent of their founders with the nimbleness and commercial sure-footedness required in such a fast-moving industry.

If this collection illustrates that it is not always easy to get all these things right, we also hope that we have demonstrated that at their best trust and charitable ownership can deliver valuable outcomes that might not otherwise be achievable. They should take on a more prominent part in the current debate about the future of news. We very much hope that this collection – which inevitably provides an incomplete version of these forms of ownership – lays the ground for a better informed debate than has been possible to date.

Biographies of Authors and Commentators

LEONARD BERKOWITZ is a director of the Thomson Reuters Founders Share Company Limited. He was previously a senior consultant with Freshfields Bruckhaus Derringer, head of the legal function at the Bank of England and a partner with Linklaters.

MANDY CORMACK is a director of the Joseph Rowntree Reform Trust and an independent advisor on corporate social responsibility. She previously worked in corporate communications and has been active in the Liberal party.

KAREN DUNLAP is president and managing director of The Poynter Institute and a member of the board of the St Petersburg Times Publishing Company and the Newspaper Association of America Foundation. She was a journalist before gaining a doctorate and becoming a faculty member at Tennessee State University and University of South Florida and then joining the Poynter Institute as faculty and becoming its dean.

NEIL FOWLER is the Guardian Research Fellow at Nuffield College, University of Oxford, and a media consultant. He was previously editor of *Which?* Magazine, publisher of *The Toronto Sun*, and an editor at several regional papers in the UK.

JOHN HONDERICH is chairman of the Torstar and the Torstar Voting Trust. He began his career in journalism at *The Ottawa Citizen* and then became a journalist, editor, and publisher of *The Toronto Star*. He has also served as chairman of Canadian Press and a director of the Canadian Newspaper Association. He is a member of the Order of Canada.

JEANNE-EMMANUELLE GAPSYS-HUTIN is a journalist at *Ouest-France* and deputy manager in charge of young readers policy.

VICTOR KEEGAN worked for forty-seven years at the *Guardian* as reporter, financial correspondent, deputy financial editor, economics editor, business editor, duty editor, chief leader writer, assistant editor, and online editor. For eleven years he was a member of the Scott Trust (owner of the *Guardian*, the *Observer* and other media interests). Until recently he wrote a weekly column on the internet and personal technology and has published several iPhone apps. In 2008 he became chairman of a not-for-profit start-up World Film Collective, which encourages youngsters in very poor countries to make and edit films with their mobiles.

DAVID A. L. LEVY is Director of the Reuters Institute for the Study of Journalism and an Associate Fellow in the Saïd Business School at University of Oxford.

CHARLES 'CHUCK' LEWIS is a tenured professor of journalism at the American University School of Communication in Washington, DC, and the founding executive editor of the Investigative Reporting Workshop there. A national investigative journalist since 1977, Lewis founded the Center for Public Integrity and several other non-profit organisations. While at the Center, he was the principal co-author of five books, including national bestseller *The Buying of the President 2004*. In late 1997, he began the Center's International Consortium of Investigative Journalists, the world's first working network of 100 premier reporters in fifty countries producing content across borders. He is a recipient of a MacArthur Fellowship and has been a fellow at the Shorenstein Center at the John F. Kennedy school of Government at Harvard University.

RASMUS KLEIS NIELSEN is assistant professor of communications at Roskilde University and research fellow at the Reuters Institute for the Study of Journalism at University of Oxford.

NIC NEWMAN is a digital strategist and consultant and a Visiting Fellow at the Reuters Institute. He was previously the future media and technology controller for BBC journalism.

ROBERT G. PICARD is Director of Research at the Reuters Institute at University of Oxford. He is the author of twenty-five books. He is editor of the *Journal of Media Business Studies* and was previously editor of the *Journal of Media Economics*. Professor Picard received his Ph.D. from the University of Missouri, Columbia, and has been a fellow at the Shorenstein Center at the John F. Kennedy School of Government at Harvard University.

JUAN SENOR is a partner at Innovation Media Consulting. He was previously a Visiting Fellow at Reuters Institute for the Study of Journalism at University of Oxford. He previously worked for International Herald Tribune Television, Wall Street Journal TV and CNBC Europe, and PBS NewsHour.

LENKA SETKOVA As Director of the Democracy and Civil Society Programme at the Carnegie UK Trust, Lenka Setkova led the Inquiry into the Future of Civil Society in the UK and Ireland, which explored the current and possible future roles of civil society in democratising news media ownership and content. Prior to this Lenka worked at New Philanthropy Capital and the Tudor Trust in the UK and at the Charles Stewart Mott Foundation and the Overseas Development Agency/Foreign and Commonwealth Office in Central and Eastern Europe.

MONIQUE VILLA is Chief Executive Officer of the Thomson Reuters Foundation. She was previously Director of Reuters Media and chairman of Action Images. Earlier she held a variety of journalistic and managerial positions with Agence France-Presse.